The Mother Tongue
Student Workbook 1

George Lyman Kittredge
Sarah Louise Arnold

Adapted By
Amy M. Edwards and Christina J. Mugglin

BLUE SKY
DAISIES

The Mother Tongue Student Workbook 1
By Amy M. Edwards and Christina J. Mugglin © 2014
Second printing, 2015

Exercises from *The Mother Tongue: Book II*
by George Lyman Kittredge, Sarah Louise Arnold © 1901, 1908

Published by Blue Sky Daisies
blueskydaisies.net

Cover design: © Blue Sky Daises 2021
ISBN-13: 978-0-9905529-1-8
ISBN-10: 0990552918

THE MOTHER TONGUE
Adapted for Modern Students
STUDENT WORKBOOK 1

The exercises in this book accompany the lessons in the text *The Mother Tongue, Adapted for Modern Students* by Amy M. Edwards and Christina J. Mugglin. The workbook exercises are presented in a format designed to make it easier for students to complete in their books. *Student Workbook 1* includes exercises for chapters 1-75.

Table of Contents

Chapter 1: General Principles

There are no written exercises given for chapter 1.

Chapter 2: The Parts of Speech

There are no written exercises given for chapter 2.

Chapter 3: Nouns

In the following passages pick out as many nouns as you can find, and tell whether each is a common or a proper noun. **Underline** the nouns and **label** the word **C** for common or **P** for proper.

1. Drake with his one ship and eighty men held boldly on; and, passing the Straits of Magellan, untraversed as yet by any Englishman, swept the unguarded coast of Chili and Peru, and loaded his bark with gold-dust and silver-ingots of Potosi, and with the pearls, emeralds, and diamonds which formed the cargo of the great galleon that sailed once a year from Lima to Cadiz.

2. In that same village, and in one of these very houses (which, to tell the precise truth, was sadly time-worn and weather-beaten), there lived many years since, while the country was yet a province of Great Britain, a simple, good-natured fellow, of the name of Rip Van Winkle. He was a descendant of the Van Winkles who figured so gallantly in the chivalrous days of Peter Stuyvesant and accompanied him to the siege of Fort Christina.

3. An inhabitant of Truro told me that about a fortnight after the St. John was wrecked at Cohasset, he found two bodies on the shore at the Clay Pounds.

4. Oliver Goldsmith was born on the tenth of November, 1728 at the hamlet of Pallas, or Pallasmore, county of Longford, in Ireland.

Chapter 4: Special Classes of Nouns

I.

In the following passages pick out all the abstract and all the collective nouns that you can find. **Underline** the nouns and **label** the word **A** for abstract or **C** for collective.

1. A number of young people were assembled in the music room.

2. He leads towards Rome a band of warlike Goths.

3. By ten o'clock the whole party were assembled at the Park.

4. Have I not reason to look pale and dead?

5. People were terrified by the force of their own imagination.

6. The Senate has letters from the general.

7. You misuse the reverence of your place.

8. There is hardly any place, or any company, where you may not gain knowledge if you please.

9. Here comes another troop to seek for you.

10. Their mastiffs are of unmatchable courage.

11. Our family dined in the field, and we sat, or rather reclined, round a temperate repast.

12. Our society will not break up, but we shall settle in some other place.

13. Let nobody blame him; his scorn I approve.

14. The Senate have concluded

    To give this day a crown to mighty Caesar.

15. He is banished, as enemy to the people and his country.

16. Society has been called the happiness of life.

17. His army is a ragged multitude

    Of hinds and peasants, rude and merciless.

18. There is a great difference between knowledge and wisdom.

19. All the country in a general voice cried hate upon him.

20. The king hath called his Parliament.

21. Let all the number of the stars give light to thy fair way!

II.

Give some **collective noun** which stands for a number or group of something. Thus,

Men — A company of men

men_____	musicians_____
birds _____	robbers _____
cows _____	pirates_____
thieves _____	books _____
marbles_____	postage stamps _____
school children _____	senators _____
sailors_____	Members of Congress _____
soldiers_____	partners in business _____
football players_____	

III.

Give an **abstract noun** which names the idea or quality suggested by each of the words in the following list. Thus,

True — The abstract noun is *truth*.   *Hasty* — The abstract noun is *haste*.

true _____	insane _____
false _____	passionate _____
good _____	natural _____
bad _____	hasty _____
lazy _____	valiant _____
careless_____	angry _____
free _____	grieving _____
brave_____	sorry _____
sinful_____	holy_____
cautious _____	evil _____
just _____	unjust _____
beautiful_____	accurate _____
amiable_____	simple_____

Chapter 5: Pronouns

I.
In the following passages **underline** the nouns and pronouns you can find. Write an **N** for noun and **P** for pronoun above the word. If you can, tell what noun is replaced by each pronoun by **drawing an arrow** from the pronoun to the noun.

1. Goneril, the elder, declared that she loved her father more than words could give out, that he was dearer to her than the light of her own eyes.

2. Bassanio took the ring and vowed never to part with it.

3. The floor of the cave was dry and level, and had a sort of small loose gravel upon it.

4. Having now brought all my things on shore, and secured them, I went back to my boat, and rowed, or paddled her along the shore, to her old harbor, where I laid her up. — *Robinson Crusoe.*

5. Heaven lies about us in our infancy.

6. Blessed is he who has found his work.

7. In fact, Tom declared it was of no use to work on his farm; it was the most pestilent little piece of ground in the whole country; everything about it went wrong, and would go wrong, in spite of him.

8. When Portia parted with her husband, she spoke cheeringly to him, and bade him bring his dear friend along with him when he returned.

II.
Fill in the blanks with pronouns.

1. A thought struck _____, and _____ wrote a letter to one of _____ friends.

2. The flowers were bending _____ heads, as if _____ were dreaming of the rainbow and dew.

3. We make way for the man who boldly pushes past _____.

4. "That's a brave man," said Wellington, when _____ saw a soldier turn pale as _____ marched against a battery: " _____ knows _____ danger, and faces _____ ."

5. I know not what course others may take; but, as for _____ , give _____ liberty, or give ____ death.

6. There, in _____ noisy mansion, skilled to rule,

    The village master taught _____ little school.

7. Wordsworth helps us to live _____ best and highest life; _____ is a strengthening and purifying influence like _____ own mountains.

8. As the queen hesitated to pass on, young Raleigh, throwing _____ cloak from his shoulder, laid _____ on the miry spot, so as to ensure _____ stepping over _____ dryshod.

9. Tender-handed stroke a nettle,

    And _____ stings you for _____ pains;

    Grasp _____ like a man of mettle,

    And _____ soft as silk remains.

10. Whatever people may think of _____ , do that which _____ believe to be right.

11. No man is so foolish but _____ may give another good counsel sometimes, and no man so wise but _____ may easily err.

Chapter 6: Verbs and Verb Phrases

I.

In each of the following passages pick out all the verbs and verb phrases that you can find. **Underline** them **twice.**

1. Count Otto stares till his eyelids ache.

2. But so slowly did I creep along, that I heard a clock in a cottage strike four before I turned down the lane from Slough to Eton.

3. Like as the waves make towards the pebbled shore,

   So do our minutes hasten to their end.

4. If it rains, we converse within doors.

5. The book you mention lies now upon my table.

6. The fleet in the Downs sent their captains on shore, hoisted the King's pennon, and blockaded the Thames.

7. The little company of the "Pilgrim Fathers," as after-times loved to call them, landed on the barren coast of Massachusetts, at a spot to which they gave the name of Plymouth, in memory of the last English port at which they touched.

II.

Pick out all the verbs and verb phrases that you can find from Chapter 5, Exercise II. **Underline** them **twice.**

III.

Fill in each blank with a verb or verb phrase.

A young friend of mine _____ a clever little dog, whose name _____ Jack. He _____ his master whenever he _____ to school, and always _____ for him until the children _____. Then the dog _____ along at the boy's heels until home _____ in sight. Once some rascal _____ Jack and _____ him up in a cellar a long way from home. But Jack _____ and _____ his master again. I never _____ a dog that _____ on his hind legs so gracefully as my friend's Jack.

Chapter 7: Sentences

I.

Make a short statement about each of the persons and things mentioned in the list below. Thus,

> *Lions* Lions are found in Africa.
> *Tree* A large tree grew in the square.

1. ball _____

2. kite _____

3. top _____

4. doll _____

5. carriage _____

6. dogs _____

7. cats _____

8. schoolhouse _____

9. John _____

10. Mary _____

11. tigers _____

12. fisherman _____

13. carpenters _____

14. book _____

15. history _____

16. sugar _____

17. leather _____

18. vinegar _____

19. apples _____

20. plums _____

21. melon _____

22. salt _____

Chapter 8: Sentences: Subject and Predicate

I.

Fill in the blanks with verbs, verb phrases, nouns, or pronouns, so as to make each example a complete sentence. **Label** the words that you supplied with **V** for verbs, **N** for nouns, or **P** for pronouns.

1. The teacher _____ at her desk writing.

2. The captain _____ his company in the suburbs of the town.

3. The strife _____ with unremitting fury for three mortal hours.

4. The first permanent settlement on the Chesapeake _____ in the beginning of the reign of James the First.

5. I _____ an aged beggar in my walk.

6. The English army _____ too exhausted for pursuit.

7. The owls _____ all night long.

8. A crow _____ a nest in one of the young elm trees.

9. A famous man _____ Robin Hood.

10. In the confusion, five or six of the enemy _____.

11. The eyes of the savage _____ with fury.

12. A little leak _____ a great ship.

13. The blacksmith _____ the red-hot iron.

14. A sudden _____ clouded the sky.

15. My _____ was then in London.

16. The _____ followed us over the moor.

17. _____ commanded the American army.

18. The _____ have wandered about nearly all day.

19. A high _____ blew hats and bonnets about.

20. The _____ fired a broadside at the enemy.

21. Many _____ were swimming in the pool.

22. Down _____ the timber with a crash.

23. Higher and higher _____ the sun.

II.

By means of a vertical line **divide** each of your completed sentences in **I,** above, into subject and predicate.

For example: The teacher | _____ at her desk writing.

Chapter 9: Complete and Simple Subject and Predicate

By means of a vertical line **divide** the following sentences into their complete subjects and complete predicates.

In each sentence point out the substantive that is the simple subject and the verb or verb phrase that is the simple predicate. **Underline** the simple subject **once** and the simple predicate **twice**. The first sentence is done for you.

1. She | roams the dreary waste.

2. Ten thousand warblers cheer the day.

3. Thou climbest the mountain-top.

4. The river glideth at his own sweet will.

5. The rings of iron sent out a jarring sound.

6. The bolted gates flew open at the blast.

7. The streets ring with clamors.

8. The courser pawed the ground with restless feet.

9. Envy can never dwell in noble hearts.

10. His whole frame was trembling.

11. The wondering stranger round him gazed.

Chapter 10: The Copula (Linking Verb) "Is"

I.

Make the following groups of words into sentences by inserting some form of the copula (*is, are,* etc.).

1. Fishes cold-blooded animals. _____

_____

2. Milton a great poet._____

_____

3. Washington the Father of his Country. _____

_____

4. You studious children. _____

_____

5. Thou the man. _____

_____

6. You a studious child._____

_____

7. He a colonel._____

_____

II.

Find the copula and **circle** it. Tell what it connects by **underlining** the words connected by the copula.

1. The stranger is an Austrian.
2. Your friends will be glad to see you.
3. We shall be too tired to walk home.
4. Seals are amphibious animals.
5. I am an American citizen.
6. The streets were wet and muddy.

7. Platinum is a very heavy metal.

8. Washington had been an officer under Braddock.

9. The Indians on Cape Cod were friendly.

10. We have been careless.

11. Sidney Lanier was a native of Georgia.

Chapter 11: Interrogative Sentences, Part 1

I.

1. Ask questions about ten objects in the schoolroom.

_____

_____

_____

_____

_____

_____

_____

_____

2. Ask ten questions about some person or event famous in American history.

_____

_____

_____

_____

_____

_____

_____

_____

3. You have just made a number of **interrogative sentences**. Write an answer to each. These answers will be **declarative sentences**.

_____

_____

_____

_____

_____

_____

_____

_____

_____

II.

Turn the following declarative sentences into interrogative sentences.

1. Our society meets once a fortnight._____

_____

2. Wellington defeated Napoleon at Waterloo. _____

_____

3. They heard the din of the battle. _____

_____

4. Swift wrote "Gulliver's Travels." _____

_____

5. Shakespeare lived in the sixteenth and seventeenth centuries._____

_____

6. Our voyage was very prosperous._____

_____

7. Nothing dries more quickly than a tear._____

_____

8. Sir John Franklin perished in the Arctic regions._____

_____

9. The Hudson's Bay Company deals in furs. _____

_____

10. John Adams was the second President of the United States._____

_____

11. Victoria is Empress of India. _____

_____

12. William II is the German Emperor. _____

_____

13. Siberia is a part of the Russian Empire. _____

_____

III.
Compare the declarative and the interrogative sentences that you have made in Exercises I and II.

Do you observe any difference in the order of words? _____

With what words do many questions begin? _____

See if you can frame a rough-and-ready rule for interrogative sentences._____

_____

Chapter 12: Interrogative Sentences, Part 2

I.

Write ten interrogative sentences beginning with *do, does,* or *did.* Use as subjects some of the nouns in the lists below.

EXAMPLES: Does Henry skate well?
Do bananas grow in Africa?

1. Henry _____

2. Washington _____

3. Julia _____

4. river _____

5. lake _____

6. mountain _____

7. ship _____

8. England _____

9. Mr. Jackson _____

10. Lowell _____

11. bananas _____

12. coconuts _____

13. children _____

14. whales _____

15. lion _____

16. cotton _____

17. breadfruit _____

18. Kansas _____

19. Henry Clay _____

Write an answer to each of your questions.

1. _____

2. _____

3. _____

4. _____

5. _____

6. _____

7. _____

8. _____

9. _____

10. _____

11. _____

12. _____

13. _____

14. _____

15. _____

16. _____

17. _____

18. _____

19. _____

II.

Write ten interrogative sentences beginning with *who, whose, whom, which,* or *what.*

1. _____

2. _____

3. _____

4. _____

5. _____

6. _____

7. _____

8. _____

9. _____

10. _____

Write answers to your questions.

11. _____

12. _____

13. _____

14. _____

15. _____

16. _____

17. _____

18. _____

19. _____

20. _____

III.

Analyze the following sentences by **underlining** the complete subject **once**, the complete predicate **twice,** and **labeling** the simple subject with an **S** and the simple predicate with a **V**. Hint: It will be easier to identify the subject if you change the question to a statement. For example, "Wealth is thy passion."

1. Is wealth thy passion?

2. What shall I say in excuse for this long letter?

3. Is he not able to pay the money?

4. Urge you your petitions in the street?

5. Why was James driven from the throne?

6. Is this the welcome of my worthy deeds?

7. Why dost thou bend thine eyes upon the earth?

8. Why do you treat Alfred Burnham so defiantly?

9. Did you ever read anything so delightful?

10. Why would not you speak sooner?

11. Does this garden belong to the governor?

Chapter 13: Imperative Sentences

I.

Make ten sentences expressing command or entreaty. How do the imperative sentences which you have made differ in form from declarative sentences?

1. _____

2. _____

3. _____

4. _____

5. _____

6. _____

7. _____

8. _____

9. _____

10. _____

II.

Make ten imperative sentences beginning with *do not*.
Observe that this is the common form of a **prohibition** (or negative command).

1. _____

2. _____

3. _____

4. _____

5. _____

6. _____

7. _____

8. _____

9. _____

10. _____

III.

Analyze the following imperative sentences:

> (1) **Underline** the subject **once**. If the subject is an implied *you* be sure to write *you* to the left of the sentence.
>
> (2) **Underline** the complete predicate **twice**.
>
> (3) **Label** the simple predicate with a **V.**

1. Go you before to Gloucester with these letters.

2. Follow thou the flowing river.

3. Go you into the other street.

4. Tomorrow in the battle think on me.

5. Do not lay your hand on your sword.

6. Bring forth the prisoners instantly.

7. Lend favorable ears to our request.

8. Call thou my brother hither.

9. Do not seek for trouble.

10. Spare my guiltless wife and my poor children.

11. See the wild waste of all-devouring years.

12. Don't measure other people's corn by your own bushel.

13. Teach not thy lips such scorn.

14. Give my regards to your brother.

15. Don't forget my message.

16. Remember never to be ashamed of doing right.

17. Do not saw the air too much with your hand.

18. Keep a firm rein upon these bursts of passion.

19. Do not spur a free horse.

20. Do not stand in your own light.

Chapter 14: Exclamatory Sentences

Identify each of the following sentences as declarative, interrogative, or imperative. Write in the blank **D**, **Int**, or **Imp**. Be prepared to give your reasons. If any of the sentences are also exclamatory be sure to **label** them **E** as well.

_____1. Did you ever hear the streams talk to you in May, when you went a-fishing?

_____2. The white pavilions made a show,
   Like remnants of the winter snow.

_____3. But hark! what means yon faint halloo?

_____4. Things are stagnant enough in town.

_____5. But what's the use of delaying?

_____6. The Moors from forth the greenwood came riding one by one.

_____7. I was just planning a whole week's adventure for you.

_____8. At the Peckham end there were a dozen handsome trees, and under them a piece of
   artificial water where boys were sailing toy boats, and a poodle was swimming.

_____9. Look at the splendid prize that was to recompense our labor.

_____10. Don't think that my temper is hot.

_____11. The natives came by degrees to be less apprehensive of any danger from me.

_____12. Soldier, rest! thy warfare o'er,
   Sleep the sleep that knows not breaking.

_____13. How easily you seem to get interested in new people!

_____14. How little I thought what the quarrel would lead to!

_____15. How have you been employing your time?

_____16. "O, cease your sports," Earl Percy said,
   "And take your bows with speed."

_____17. He had been in business in the West End.

_____18. Abandon this mad enterprise.

_____19. Forgive my hasty words.

_____20. What black despair, what horror, fills his heart!

Chapter 15: Vocative

I.

Fill in the blanks with **vocatives**. Observe that each sentence is complete already, and that the vocatives are not necessary to the thought.

1. We shall miss you very much,_____.

2. Come hither,_____, and sit upon my knee.

3. What is your name,_____?

4. _____, can you tell me the road to Denver ?

5. _____, spare that tree.

6. Don't disappoint me,_____. I trust you absolutely.

7. Jog on,_____, and we shall soon reach the stable.

8. Run,_____! The savages are after us!

9. Swim,_____, for your life. There's a shark chasing you!

10. Jump, _____! It's our last chance!

II.

In each of the following sentences **underline** the complete subject **once** and the complete predicate **twice**. Remember that vocatives stand alone and are not part of either the complete subject *or* the complete predicate. Also **label** any vocative nouns which the sentences contain with a **V**.

1. O learned sir,

    You and your learning I revere.

2. The good old man

    Means no offense, sweet lady!

3. Goodbye! Drive on, coachman.

4. Why, Sir John, my face does you no harm.

5. Good cousin, give me audience for a while.

6. Yours is the prize, victorious prince.

7. "Wake, Allan-bane," aloud she cried

    To the old minstrel by her side.

8. Bid adieu, my sad heart, bid adieu to thy peace.

9. My dear little cousin, what can be the matter?

10. Come, Evening, once again, season of peace!

11. Plain truth, dear Murray, needs no flowers of speech.

12. Permit me now, Sir William, to address myself personally to you.

13. Go, my dread lord, to your great-grandsire's tomb.

14. Why do you stay so long, my lords of France?

15. My pretty cousins, you mistake me much.

16. Come on, Lord Hastings. Will you go with me?

17. O Romeo, Romeo, brave Mercutio's dead.

18. I will avenge this insult, noble queen.

19. O friend, I seek a harborage for the night.

20. My lord, I saw three bandits by the rock.

21. Father! thy days have passed in peace.

III.

(1) Identify each of the following sentences as declarative, interrogative, or imperative. Write in the blank **D**, **Int**, or **Imp**.
(2) **Divide** each into the complete subject and the complete predicate with a vertical line. **Underline** the simple subject **once** and the simple predicate **twice**.
(3) **Label** any vocatives that you find with a **V**.

_____1. I had a violent fit of the nightmare.

_____2. It was at the time of the annual fair.

_____3. My uncle was an old traveler.

_____4. The young lady closed the casement with a sigh.

_____5. The supper table was at length laid.

_____6. Hoist out the boat.

_____7. Are you from the farm?

_____8. She broke into a little scornful laugh.

_____9. Bring forth the horse.

_____10. When can their glory fade?

_____11. Shut, shut the door, good John!

_____12. Do you mark that, my lord?

_____13. Why sigh you so profoundly?

_____14. Within the mind strong fancies work.

_____15. The sun peeps gay at dawn of day.

_____16. The noble stag was pausing now

Upon the mountain's southern brow.

_____17. Then through the dell his horn resounds.

_____18. Lightly and brightly breaks away

The Morning from her mantle gray.

_____19. Fire flashed from out the old Moor's eyes.

_____20. The garlands wither on their brow.

IV.

Change the declarative sentences in Exercise III, above, into interrogative sentences. What changes do you make in the **form** of each sentence?

1. _____

2. _____

3. _____

4. _____

5. _____

6. _____

7. _____

8. _____

9. _____

10. _____

11. _____

12. _____

13. _____

14. _____

15. _____

16. _____

17. _____

18. _____

19. _____

20. _____

Chapter 16: Adjectives

I.
Circle the adjectives and **draw an arrow** to the noun or pronoun that it modifies.

1. The sun is warm, the sky is clear.

2. Hope must have green bowers and blue skies.

3. His axe is keen, his arm is strong.

4. La Fleur instantly pulled out a little dirty pocket-book, crammed full of small letters.

5. His white hair floats like a snowdrift around his face.

6. A sorrowful multitude followed them to the shore.

7. My fugitive years are all hasting away.

8. The sails of this vessel are black.

9. The old officer was reading a small pamphlet.

10. He was almost frantic with grief.

11. We are weak and miserable.

12. A more striking picture there could not be imagined than the beautiful English face of the girl, and its exquisite bloom, together with her erect and independent attitude, contrasted with the sallow and bilious skin of the Malay, veneered with mahogany tints by climate and marine air, his small, fierce, restless eyes, thin lips, slavish gestures and adorations.

II.
Fill in each blank with an **adjective** limiting the simple subject of the sentence.

1. A _____ palace rose before us.

2. A _____ path led down to the brook.

3. _____ Indians attacked the village.

4. The _____ soldier was severely wounded.

5. _____ boys threw stones at the train.

6. A _____ lamp was burning in the room.

7. A _____ tower stood on the cliff.

8. Two _____ dogs guarded the house.

9. The _____ pupil has forgotten his book.

10. _____ walls surrounded the garden.

11. The _____ elephant seized his tormentor.

12. This _____ merchant lived in Chicago.

III.

Complete each sentence by filling the blank with a **noun** as simple subject. Make sure that your choice makes sense with the adjectives given.

1. A fierce _____ sprang at the beggar.

2. Envious _____ are never happy.

3. The cowardly _____ deserted his companion.

4. A heavy _____ fell from the staging.

5. A bright _____ blazed on the hearth.

6. Smooth _____ covered the sidewalk.

7. A golden _____ was on his head.

8. Many _____ make light work.

9. My faithful _____ never left me.

10. Dark _____ shut out the sun.

11. A cold _____ is blowing.

12. The tall _____ was covered with snow.

13. A soft _____ turneth away wrath.

14. Angry _____ seldom give good advice.

15. Four black _____ drew the coach.

Chapter 17: Classes of Adjectives

I.
Fill the blanks with appropriate **adjectives**.

1. Spring is cheery, but winter is _____.

2. A _____ fairy comes at night. Her eyes are _____, her hair is _____.

3. The _____ castle had never held half so many _____ knights beneath its roof.

4. Holly is _____ in the winter.

5. No _____ fire blazed on the hearth.

6. Wellington was an _____ general.

7. I wish you a _____ New Year.

8. Down he sank in the _____ waves.

9. The clothes and food of the children are _____ and _____.

10. His eyes are _____ with weeping.

11. "'Twas a _____ victory," said the _____ man.

12. _____ snow lay on the ground.

13. No footstep marked the _____ gravel.

14. Miss Bell seemed very _____.

15. John looks as _____ as a judge.

II.
Make twenty sentences, each containing one of these adjectives followed by a noun.

1. proud _____

2. tall _____

3. rusty _____

4. ruinous _____

5. anxious _____

6. careless _____

7. faithful _____

8. angry _____

9. blue-eyed _____

10. plentiful _____

11. purple _____

12. flowery _____

13. outrageous _____

14. accurate _____

15. fault-finding _____

16. swift _____

17. patriotic _____

18. athletic _____

19. torrid _____

20. American _____

III.

Mention a number of adjectives that might be used in describing each of the following objects.

1. iron _____

2. lead _____

3. robin _____

4. parrot _____

5. eagle _____

6. sparrow _____

7. bicycle _____

8. horse _____

9. oxen _____

10. cornfield _____

11. spring _____

12. summer _____

13. autumn_____

14. winter_____

15. butterfly_____

16. spider _____

17. carpenter _____

18. physician _____

19. sugar_____

20. marble _____

IV.

Use in a sentence each of the nouns in the list below. With each noun use an adjective. Thus,

Noun: *dog*   Adjective: *shaggy*
Sentence: That *shaggy dog* of John's needs clipping.

1. cat _____

2. engineer _____

3. game_____

4. hall _____

5. orange _____

6. lemon _____

7. sailor_____

8. architect _____

9. president _____

10. Washington _____

11. scholar _____

12. mechanic _____

13. board _____

14. saw _____

15. book _____

16. merchant _____

17. battle_____

18. charge_____

19. artillery _____

20. grove _____

21. prairie_____

22. mountain _____

23. lake _____

Chapter 18: The Two Articles

I.

Underline the indefinite articles in the following passages, and observe whether the form is *a* or *an*.

1. Whenever there was sickness in the place, she was an untiring nurse.

2. We are going to have a great archery party next month, and you shall have an invitation.

3. But man of all ages is a selfish animal, and unreasonable in his selfishness.

4. There is a pleasure in the pathless woods.

5. At length I met a reverend good old man.

6. He was lying on a crimson velvet sofa, reading a French novel. It was a very little book. He is a very little man. In that enormous hall he looked like a mere speck.

II.

In the following sentences supply an **article**, either definite or indefinite. In case it is possible to supply either the definite or the indefinite article, tell what difference of meaning comes from using one rather than the other.

1. The schoolhouse was _____ low building rudely constructed of logs; _____ windows were partly glazed, and partly patched with leaves of old copybooks.

2. He was always ready for either _____ fight or _____ frolic.

3. It was, as I have said, _____ fine autumnal day. _____ sky was clear and serene.

4. _____ sloop was loitering in _____ distance, dropping slowly down with _____ tide, her sail hanging uselessly against _____ mast.

5. _____ musician was _____ old gray-headed negro.

6. On one side of _____ church extends a wide woody dell, along which raves _____ large brook.

III.

In the following passage, point out all the definite and all the indefinite articles and tell to what noun each belongs. **Label** the definite articles with a **D** and the indefinite with an **I**. **Draw an arrow** to the noun to which it belongs.

1. An acquaintance, a friend as he called himself, entered.

2. The town was in a hubbub.

3. The men were quiet and sober.

4. You see this man about whom so great an uproar hath been made in this town.

5. I disliked carrying a musket.

6. I sat down on one of the benches, at the other end of which was seated a man in very shabby clothes.

7. The ploughman whistles.

8. The mower whets his scythe.

9. Young and old come forth to play

    On a sunshine holiday.

Chapter 19: Adverbs

I.

Pick out the adverbs and tell what verb or verb phrase each modifies. **Circle** the adverbs and **underline** the verb or verb phrase twice. **Draw an arrow** from the adverb to the verb.

1. Carroll waved his whip triumphantly in the air.

2. This contemptuous speech cruelly shocked Cecilia.

3. Spring came upon us suddenly.

4. The king gained ground everywhere.

5. Every night in dreams they groaned aloud.

6. Northward he turneth through a little door.

7. I dimly discerned a wall before me.

8. Miss Sharp had demurely entered the carriage some minutes before.

9. Punctuality at meals was rigidly enforced at Gateshead Hall.

10. But here the doctors eagerly dispute.

11. The guardsman defended himself bravely.

12. Swiftly, swiftly flew the ship,

    Yet she sailed softly too:

    Sweetly, sweetly blew the breeze —

    On me alone it blew.

13. Kent had been looking at me steadily for some time.

14. By this storm our ship was greatly damaged.

II.

Change the meaning of each of the following sentences by substituting a different adverb.

1. Stevens laughed boisterously.

_____

2. Merrily sang the birds in the wood.

_____

3. You have acted unjustly toward your brother.

_____

4. The ship settled in the water gradually.

_____

5. Fiercely the chieftain made reply.

_____

6. We rowed slowly up the stream.

_____

7. Mr. Fleetwood entered the room noisily.

_____

8. They waited patiently for better times.

_____

III.

Fill in each blank with an **adverb** and **draw** an arrow to the word it modifies.

1. This poor fellow has been _____ hurt.

2. All the pupils were _____ delighted with the entertainment.

3. The explosion did _____ great damage.

4. Joe passed his hand _____ over his aching forehead.

5. The prisoner struggled _____.

6. _____ many objections were heard.

7. I am not _____ unhappy, but still I am _____ uncomfortable.

8. Helen speaks _____ rapidly; John does not speak rapidly _____.

9. The wind howled _____ down the wide chimney.

10. My boat will hold six persons _____.

11. The room is not large _____ for the class.

12. The scout crept _____ through the thicket.

13. Jackson's salary is _____ small for his needs.

14. The river is rising _____ rapidly.

15. Such conduct will be _____ punished.

Chapter 20: Adverbs Modifying Adjectives

Circle the adverbs that modify adjectives and **draw an arrow** to the adjective it modifies.

1. Her language is singularly agreeable to me.

2. Mr. Sedley's eyes twinkled in a manner indescribably roguish.

3. The river walk is uncommonly pretty.

4. She had been going on a bitterly cold winter night to visit some one at Stamford Hill.

5. Mrs. Harrel was extremely uneasy.

6. The meeting was very painful to them both.

7. Kate had been unreasonably angry with Heatherleigh.

8. Be particularly careful not to stumble.

9. The poor fellow was pitifully weak.

Chapter 21: Adverbs Modifying Adverbs

Circle the adverbs that modify other adverbs and **draw an arrow** to the adverb it modifies.

1. She told her distress quite frankly.

2. Cecilia then very gravely began an attempt to undeceive her.

3. This service she somewhat reluctantly accepted.

4. He fixed his eyes on me very steadily.

5. We strolled along rather carelessly towards Hampstead.

6. Do not speak so indistinctly.

7. The red horse trots uncommonly fast.

8. The commander rebuked his boldness half seriously, half jestingly.

9. The cotton must be picked pretty soon.

10. Why did King Lear's daughters treat him so unkindly?

Chapter 22: Classification of Adverbs

I.

Fill in each blank with an **adverb of degree** and tell how it modifies the adjective or the adverb that follows.

1. The wind blew _____ hard.

2. The air bites shrewdly; it is _____ cold.

3. I was in the utmost astonishment, and roared _____ loud that they all ran back in

   fright.

4. I bowed _____ respectfully to the governor.

5. The peacock's voice is not _____ beautiful as his plumage.

6. We jogged homeward merrily _____.

7. Tom was _____ angry to measure his words.

8. The load was _____ too heavy for the horse to draw.

9. "My lesson is _____ hard. Is yours?" "No, not very; but still it is _____

   difficult."

10. The physician was rather surprised to find his patient _____ lively.

11. This has been an _____ dry season.

II.

Very many adverbs end in *-ly*. These are usually derived from adjectives. Thus,

ADJECTIVES	ADVERBS
fair	fairly
bold	boldly
cordial	cordially
outrageous	outrageously

Form **adverbs** from the adjectives in the following list. Use each adverb in a sentence.

1. fine _____

   _____

2. courageous _____

   _____

3. brave _____

   _____

4. splendid _____

   _____

5. eager _____

   _____

6. plain _____

   _____

7. doubtful _____

   _____

8. confusing _____

   _____

9. remarkable _____

   _____

10. heedless _____

   _____

11. careful _____

_____

12. polite _____

_____

13. rude _____

_____

14. civil _____

_____

15. violent _____

_____

16. mild _____

_____

17. meek _____

_____

18. gentle _____

_____

19. smooth _____

_____

20. soft _____

_____

21. boisterous _____

_____

III.

In the sentences which you have made in Exercise II, tell whether the adverb modifies a verb, an adjective, or another adverb.

1. _____   12. _____

2. _____   13. _____

3. _____   14. _____

4. _____   15. _____

5. _____   16. _____

6. _____   17. _____

7. _____   18. _____

8. _____   19. _____

9. _____   20. _____

10. _____ 21. _____

11. _____

IV.

Use each of the following verbs and verb phrases with several different adverbs, and see how the meaning varies. Let each of your examples be a sentence.

1. sings _____

_____

2. runs _____

_____

3. flies _____

_____

4. talks _____

_____

5. walks _____

_____

6. works _____

_____

7. acted _____

_____

8. spent_____

_____

9. played_____

_____

10. rushes_____

_____

11. has confessed _____

_____

12. were marching _____

_____

13. are writing_____

_____

14. gazed _____

_____

15. have examined _____

_____

16. will study_____

_____

17. devoured _____

_____

18. shall watch_____

_____

19. may hurt _____

_____

20. can ride _____

_____

21. has injured_____

_____

22. will attack _____

_____

V.

Read the sentences which you have made in Exercise IV, omitting all the adverbs. Observe how this changes the meaning.

VI.

Pick out all the adverbs in chapter 19, Exercises I and II. Tell whether they are adverbs of **time, place, manner,** or **degree**, and indicate what **verb, adjective,** or **adverb** each modifies.

NOTE: In determining whether an adverb indicates **manner, time, place,** or **degree**, the student will do well to test the matter by asking himself whether the word answers the question *"how?" "when?" "where?"* or *"to what extent?"*

I.

1. _____   8. _____

2. _____   9. _____

3. _____   10. _____

4. _____   11. _____

5. _____   12. _____

6. _____   13. _____

7. _____   14. _____

II.

1. _____   5. _____

2. _____   6. _____

3. _____   7. _____

4. _____   8. _____

VII.

For each adverb in the sentences in chapter 19, Exercises I and II, **substitute** some other adverb.

Observe what effect this change has on the meaning of each sentence.

I.
1. _____

2. _____

3. _____

4. _____

5. _____

6. _____

7. _____

8. _____

9. _____

10. _____

11. _____

12. _____

13. _____

14. _____

II.
1. _____

2. _____

3. _____

4. _____

5. _____

6. _____

7. _____

8. _____

Chapter 23: Analysis: Modifiers

I.

Analyze the sentences below, as follows:

      (1) **Underline** the simple subject **once** and the simple predicate **twice**.

      (2) **Divide** each sentence into the complete subject and the complete predicate with a vertical line.

      (3) **Label** any adjectives, including articles, that modify the subject with **Adj**.

      (4) **Label** any adverbs that modify the predicate with **Adv**.

1. The large room was quickly filled.

2. A great wood fire blazed cheerfully.

3. Our dusty battalions marched onward.

4. The heavy gates were shut instantly.

5. A magnificent snow-fed river poured ceaselessly through the glen.

6. Back darted Spurius Lartius.

7. A meager little man was standing near.

8. This terrible winter dragged slowly along.

9. The cattle were feeding quietly.

10. Instantly a dire hubbub arose.

11. The red sun sank slowly behind the hills.

12. Many strange stories were told of this adventure.

II.

Expand the following short sentences by **inserting** modifiers of the subject and of the predicate.

1. Men work. _____

2. Pupils studied. _____

3. The wind howls. _____

4. Women were weeping. _____

5. Grapes hung. _____

6. Enemy resisted. _____

7. Crows were cawing._____

8. Corn grew. _____

9. Fire spread. _____

10. Messenger rode. _____

11. Building fell. _____

12. Child cried. _____

13. Dog swam._____

14. Tiger sprang. _____

Chapter 24: Prepositions

I.

Fill in the blanks with **prepositions** showing the relation of the italicized words to each other.

1. John's hat *hung* _____ the *peg*.

2. The river *rises* _____ the *mountains* and *flows* _____ a great *plain* _____ the *sea*.

3. The miseries of numbed hands and shivering skins no longer accompany every *pull* _____ the river.

4. He *was* _____ a particularly *good-humor* with himself.

5. His conscience pricked him for *intruding* _____ *Hardy* during his hours of work.

6. Tom came to understand the *differences* _____ his two *heroes*.

7. Such cruelty *fills* us _____ *indignation*.

8. He was *haunted* _____ a hundred *fears*.

9. _____ a score of *minutes* Garbetts *came* back _____ an anxious and crestfallen *countenance*.

10. To *drive* the deer _____ *hound* and *horn* Earl Percy took his way.

11. Cooks, butlers, and their assistants were *bestirring* themselves _____ the *kitchen*.

12. The weary traveler *was sleeping* _____ a *tree*.

13. Jack *hid* _____ the *door*.

14. I will *call* _____ *dinner*.

II.

Use the following prepositions, with objects, in sentences:

of _____

in _____

upon _____

from _____

by _____

to _____

into _____

during _____

along _____

behind _____

within _____

without _____

till _____

up _____

down _____

round _____

at _____

beside _____

before _____

against _____

about _____

concerning _____

except _____

but (= except) _____

beyond _____

through _____

throughout _____

after _____

above _____

beneath _____

over _____

under _____

III.

In the following sentences:
   (1) **Circle** the prepositions;
   (2) **Draw an arrow** to their objects;
   (3) **Underline** the word(s) with which each preposition connects its object;
   (4) **Label** the underlined word(s) with **P** if it is a pronoun, **A** if it is an article or **Adj** for other adjectives.

1. The village maid steals through the shade.

2. His eyes burnt like coals under his deep brows.

3. Their vessels were moored in our bay.

4. The hounds ran swiftly through the woods.

5. They knocked at our gates for admittance.

6. I grew weary of the sea and intended to stay at home with my wife and family.

7. Several officers of the army went to the door of the great council chamber.

8. This seems to me but melancholy work.

9. The bowmen mustered on the hills.

10. Death lays his icy hand on kings.

11. Untie these bands from off my hands.

12. Down the wide stairs a darkling way they found.

13. He halts, and searches with his eyes

    Among the scattered rocks.

14. The cottage windows through the twilight blazed.

15. All shod with steel,

    We hissed along the polished ice.

16. He was full of joke and jest.

17. Lady Waldegrave swept her fingers over a harp which stood near.

IV.

Underline fifteen prepositions in some poem of your choice. **Circle** the object of each preposition.

"Lochinvar" by Sir Walter Scott (1771-1832) is provided for you here.

OH! young Lochinvar is come out of the west,
Through all the wide Border his steed was the best;
And save his good broadsword he weapons had none.
He rode all unarmed and he rode all alone.
So faithful in love and so dauntless in war,
There never was knight like the young Lochinvar.

He stayed not for brake and he stopped not for stone,
He swam the Eske river where ford there was none,
But ere he alighted at Netherby gate
The bride had consented, the gallant came late:
For a laggard in love and a dastard in war
Was to wed the fair Ellen of brave Lochinvar.

So boldly he entered the Netherby Hall,
Among bridesmen, and kinsmen, and brothers, and all:
Then spoke the bride's father, his hand on his sword,—
For the poor craven bridegroom said never a word,—
'Oh! come ye in peace here, or come ye in war,
Or to dance at our bridal, young Lord Lochinvar?'—

'I long wooed your daughter, my suit you denied;
Love swells like the Solway, but ebbs like its tide—
And now am I come, with this lost love of mine,
To lead but one measure, drink one cup of wine.
There are maidens in Scotland more lovely by far,
That would gladly be bride to the young Lochinvar.'

The bride kissed the goblet; the knight took it up,
He quaffed off the wine, and he threw down the cup,
She looked down to blush, and she looked up to sigh,
With a smile on her lips and a tear in her eye.
He took her soft hand ere her mother could bar,—
'Now tread we a measure!' said young Lochinvar.

So stately his form, and so lovely her face,
That never a hall such a galliard did grace;
While her mother did fret, and her father did fume,
And the bridegroom stood dangling his bonnet and plume;
And the bride-maidens whispered ''Twere better by far
To have matched our fair cousin with young Lochinvar.'

One touch to her hand and one word in her ear,
When they reached the hall-door, and the charger stood near;
So light to the croupe the fair lady he swung,
So light to the saddle before her he sprung!
'She is won! we are gone, over bank, bush, and scaur;
They'll have fleet steeds that follow,' quoth young Lochinvar.

There was mounting 'mong Graemes of the Netherby clan;
Fosters, Fenwicks, and Musgraves, they rode and they ran:
There was racing and chasing on Cannobie Lee,
But the lost bride of Netherby ne'er did they see.
So daring in love and so dauntless in war,
Have ye e'er heard of gallant like young Lochinvar?

Write the prepositional phrase on each line and note what other word is connected by the preposition to its object. The first one is done for you.

1. _"of the west"_   _"of" connects "west" to "come out"_ _____

2. _____

3. _____

4. _____

5. _____

6. _____

7. _____

8. _____

9. _____

10. _____

11. _____

12. _____

13. _____

14. _____

15. _____

Chapter 25: Conjunctions

I.

Circle the conjunctions, and **place** parentheses around the words, or groups of words, they connect.

1. The wind was high and the clouds were dark,

    And the boat returned no more.

2. It was the time when lilies blow

    And clouds are highest up in air.

3. Beating heart and burning brow, ye are very patient now.

4. The uncouth person in the tattered garments dropped on both knees on the pavement, and took her hand in his, and kissed it in passionate gratitude.

5. He rose, and stood with his cap in his hand.

6. She bowed to him, and passed on, grave and stately.

7. She was an amiable but strictly matter-of-fact person.

8. Brand became more and more convinced that this family was the most delightful family in England.

9. If there were any stranger here at all, we should not dream of asking you to sing.

10. Helen was on the lookout for this expected guest, and saw him from her window. But she did not come forward.

11. I am busy and content.

12. Carrying this fateful letter in his hand, he went downstairs and out into the cool night air.

13. For Romans in Rome's quarrel

    Spared neither land nor gold,

    Nor son nor wife, nor limb nor life,

    In the brave days of old.

14. He was neither angry nor impatient.

15. There were forty craft in Avès that were both swift and stout.

16. We knew you must come by sooner or later.

17. He continued his story, though his listener seemed singularly preoccupied and thoughtful.

II.

Make sentences containing:

1. Two nouns connected by *and*; by *or*.

    _____

    _____

2. A noun and a pronoun connected by *and*; by *or*.

    _____

    _____

3. Two adjectives connected by *and*; by *or*.

    _____

    _____

4. Two adverbs connected by *and*; by *or*.

    _____

    _____

5. Two verbs connected by *and*; by *or*.

    _____

    _____

6. Two adverbs connected by *and*; by *or*.

    _____

    _____

7. *Neither---nor* connecting nouns.

    _____

8. *Neither---nor* connecting pronouns.

    _____

9. *Neither---nor* connecting adjectives.

    _____

10. *Neither---nor* connecting adverbs.

    _____

11. *Neither---nor* connecting verbs.

    _____

12- 16. *Either---or,* used like *neither---nor* in 7-11.

12. _____

13. _____

14. _____

15. _____

16. _____

17. Three nouns in a series, with two conjunctions; with one.

_____

_____

18. Three verbs in a series, with two conjunctions; with one.

_____

_____

III.

Make sentences, each containing one of the following conjunctions:

1. and _____

2. but_____

3. or_____

4. nor _____

5. neither _____

6. if _____

7. however_____

8. although_____

9. since _____

10. for _____

11. because_____

12. whether _____

13. than_____

IV.

Find ten conjunctions in chapter 5, Exercise I, and tell what each conjunction connects.

1. _____

2. _____

3. _____

4. _____

5. _____

6. _____

7. _____

8. _____

9. _____

10. _____

V.

Fill in each blank with a **conjunction**.

1. Iron, lead, _____ gold are metals.

2. _____ Jack nor Joe is at school.

3. _____ you do not hurry, you will miss the train.

4. Either Mary _____ Francis is to blame.

5. There are _____ lions _____ tigers in the jungle.

6. _____one or the other of us must give way.

Chapter 26: Interjections

I.

In the following sentences **circle** the interjections and **write** on the blank what emotion you think each expresses.

1. Fie, fie! they are not to be named, my lord. _____

2. Pish for thee, Iceland dog! _____

3. Lo! where the giant on the mountain stands. _____

4. "Ah me!" she cries, "was ever moonlight seen so clear?" _____

5. Pshaw! this neglect is accident, and the effect of hurry. _____

6. O, let us yet be merciful. _____

7. That I did love thee, Caesar, O, 't is true. _____

8. The Wildgrave winds his bugle-horn. _____

   To horse, to horse! halloo! halloo! _____

9. But psha! I've the heart of a soldier, _____

   All gentleness, mercy, and pity. _____

10. Louder rang the Wildgrave's horn, _____

    "Hark forward, forward! holla, ho!" _____

11. Huzza for the Arethusa! She is a frigate tight and brave. _____

II.

Try to think of some **interjections** that you are in the habit of using, and frame sentences containing them.
What emotion does each express?

1. _____

2. _____

3. _____

4. _____

5. _____

Chapter 27: Phrases

I.

Make sentences of your own containing the following phrases:

1. baseball club_____

2. Queen of England _____

3. will come _____

4. has traveled _____

5. North American Continent _____

6. Isthmus of Suez _____

7. in the street_____

8. on the playground_____

9. with an effort _____

10. of fur _____

11. of silver _____

12. had tried _____

13. at sea _____

14. at home _____

15. in school _____

16. of iron _____

17. of stone _____

18. with the exception of _____

19. out of _____

20. in front of _____

21. against my will_____

II.

Label, if you can, what part of speech each of the phrases in Exercise I, above, resembles in its use in your sentence.

1. _____

2. _____

3. _____

4. _____

5. _____

6. _____

7. _____

8. _____

9. _____

10. _____

11. _____

12. _____

13. _____

14. _____

15. _____

16. _____

17. _____

18. _____

19. _____

20. _____

21. _____

III.

Identify each word's part of speech in the phrases below. The first one is done for you.

1. baseball club_____ *baseball: adjective   club: noun* _____

2. Queen of England _____

3. will come _____

4. has traveled _____

5. North American Continent _____

6. Isthmus of Suez _____

7. in the street_____

8. on the playground_____

9. with an effort _____

10. of fur _____

11. of silver _____

12. had tried _____

13. at sea _____

14. at home _____

15. in school _____

16. of iron _____

17. of stone _____

18. with the exception of _____

19. out of _____

20. in front of _____

21. against my will_____

IV.

Underline one **phrase** in each of the following sentences. **Label**, if you can, for what part of speech it stands.

1. The Declaration of Independence was signed in 1776.

2. The House of Representatives has adjourned.

3. Professor Edward Johnston is now in Sioux City.

4. The great Desert of Sahara is in the Continent of Africa.

5. All were on their feet in a moment.

6. The preparations for disembarking had begun.

7. The Pacific Mail Steamship Company has an office at this port.

8. Isabel shuddered with horror.

9. I am a man of peace, though my abode now rings with arms.

10. They were all running at full speed.

11. They had fixed the wedding day.

12. There are many thousand Cinderellas in London, and elsewhere in England.

13. The maddened, terrified horse went like the wind.

14. The Prince of Wales is heir to the crown of England.

15. "In two days," Cromwell said coolly, "the city will be in our hands."

16. The scene had now become in the utmost degree animated and horrible.

17. There were upwards of three hundred strangers in the house.

18. The dog is not of mountain breed.

19. The boys were coming out of the grammar school in shoals, laughing, running, whooping, as the manner of boys is.

20. My father walked up and down the room with impatience.

21. Mr. Thomas Inkle of London, aged twenty years, embarked in the Downs on the good ship called the Achilles, bound for the West Indies, on the 16th of June, 1647, in order to improve his fortune by trade and merchandise.

Chapter 28: Adjective Phrases

I.

Place parentheses around the adjective phrases and **draw an arrow** to the substantive each describes or limits.

1. A man of strong understanding is generally a man of strong character.

2. His flaxen hair, of sunny hue,

   Curled closely round his bonnet blue.

3. Eastward was built a gate of marble white.

4. He found a strong, fierce-looking Highlander, with an axe on his shoulder, standing

   sentinel at the door.

5. Hard by a poplar shook alway,

   All silver-green, with gnarled bark.

6. The gentleness of heaven is on the sea.

7. The balustrade of the staircase was also of carved wood.

8. Of stature fair, and slender frame,

   But firmly knit, was Malcolm Graeme.

9. It was a lodge of ample size.

10. This gentleman was a man of unquestioned courage.

11. An emperor in his nightcap would not meet with half the respect of an emperor with a

    glittering crown.

12. Our affairs are in a bad condition.

13. Yathek arose in the morning with a mind more at ease.

14. Her own mind was now in a state of the utmost confusion.

15. Griffiths was a hard business man, of shrewd, worldly good sense, but of little refinement

    or cultivation.

II.

Substitute for each italicized adjective an adjective phrase without changing the general meaning of the sentence. Thus,

> The cashier was a *strictly honest* man.
> The cashier was a man *of strict honesty.*

1. The cashier was a strictly *honest* man. ___*Answer given for you above*___

_____

2. A very *deep* ravine checked our advance. _____

_____

3. Brutus is an *honorable* man. _____

_____

4. *Wooden* pillars supported the roof. _____

_____

5. The wanderer's clothing was *ragged.* _____

_____

6. The sailor carried an *ivory-handled* knife. _____

_____

7. The runner was quite *breathless.* _____

_____

8. The baron lived in his *ancestral* castle. _____

_____

9. *Light-hearted* he rose in the morning. _____

_____

10. Dr. Rush was a *skillful* and *experienced* physician. _____

_____

III.

Place parentheses around each adjective phrase. On the blank provided, re-write the sentence replacing the adjective phrases with adjectives without materially changing the sense. The first one is done for you.

1. Warrington was (of a quick and impetuous temper.) ___*Warrington was quick-tempered.*___

2. The road was not of the most picturesque description. _____

3. Fanny left the room with a sorrowful heart. _____

4. You are a man of sense. _____

5. Upon the hero's head was a helmet of brass. _____

6. Bring forth the goblets of gold! _____

7. To scale the wall was a task of great difficulty. _____

8. The old soldier was in poverty. _____

9. We were all in high spirits. _____

10. A river of great width had to be crossed. _____

11. He told his fellow-prisoners, in this darkest time, to be of courage. _____

12. This is a matter of importance. _____

13. The beast glared at me with eyes of fire. _____

Chapter 28: Additional Exercises

I.

Analyze the sentences below, as follows:

    (1) **Underline** the complete subject **once** and the complete predicate **twice**.

    (2) **Label** the simple subject with **S**.

    (3) **Label** the simple predicate with **V**.

    (4) **Label** modifiers of the subject (adjectives and adjective phrases) with **Adj**.

1. The men of Rome hated kings.

2. A thing of beauty is a joy forever.

3. Steps of marble led up to the palace door.

4. A ladder of ropes hung from the balcony.

5. A huge nugget of gold rewarded my search.

6. A book with heavy clasps was found in the chest.

7. The sword in his hand trembled violently.

8. A figure with three angles is a triangle.

9. The heights above us were shrouded in mist.

10. An animal with four legs is called a quadruped.

11. Diamonds from Africa lay in the casket.

12. The subject under discussion was fiercely argued.

13. Rough herdsmen from the mountains filled the square.

14. My friends at home write to me seldom.

15. My uncle in London sent me an urgent message.

16. Books by the best authors were his delight.

17. The silence of the prairie was well-nigh terrible.

18. The horse chestnuts in the sheltered square broke into blossom.

19. A group of strange children ran at his heels.

20. The light on the mantel piece had burnt low.

21. The customs of mankind are influenced by climate.

22. The tree before his window was a shabby sycamore.

23. Before him rose a gate of marble white.

II.
Analyze the following sentences as in Exercise I.

1. A giant with three heads lived in the cave.

2. A man with a scythe stood in the path.

3. A poodle with shaggy hair barked on the doorstep.

4. That castle on the cliff looks very ancient.

5. His money in the bank is his dearest possession.

6. The comrade by his side fell in the first attack.

7. The portraits on the wall frowned at him.

8. The bucket in the well was old and water-soaked.

9. A big dog under the table growled and showed his teeth.

10. The path by the brook wound pleasantly along.

11. The pain in his arm grew unendurable.

12. The road to ruin is all downhill.

13. My voyage among the islands lasted three days.

14. The smile on her lips faded.

15. The road through the forest is dangerous.

16. The man at the wheel was washed overboard.

17. The workmen in the factory struck for higher wages.

Chapter 29: Adverbial Phrases

I.

Use each of the adverbial phrases in Section 127, Exercises I and II, in a sentence.
Do the same with those in Section 130.

TIME:

before long _____

in olden times_____

in youth_____

in age_____

in middle life _____

without delay _____

on the spot _____

of yore _____

of old _____

PLACE:

in town _____

away from home _____

at a distance _____

in this vicinity _____

in front _____

at one side_____

to windward_____

to the eastward_____

to and fro _____

now and then _____

up and down _____

again and again _____

first and last _____

full speed _____

full tilt _____

hit or miss _____

more or less _____

head first_____

upside down _____

inside out _____

sink or swim_____

cash down_____

II.

Here is a short list of adverbs with adverbial phrases which have the same meaning:

courageously: with courage.   furiously: with fury
eloquently: with eloquence   easily: with ease, without effort
purposely: on purpose   fearlessly: without fear
unwillingly: against his will   vainly: in vain

Write five more of your own examples on the lines provided.
Write a sentence including each of these thirteen adverbs.
Read your sentences aloud, substituting for the adverb the corresponding phrase.

_____

_____

_____

_____

_____

_____

_____

_____

_____

_____

_____

_____

_____

_____

_____

III.

Place parentheses around the adverbial phrases and **draw an arrow** to what each modifies.

1. Early in the morning a sudden storm drove us within two or three leagues of Ireland.

2. These things terrified the people to the last degree.

3. At the first glimpse of dawn he hastened to the prison.

4. The wall fell with a crash.

5. By daybreak we had sailed out of sight of land.

6. The full light of day had now risen upon the desert.

7. With smiles the rising morn we greet.

8. Innumerable dismal stories we heard every day.

9. Homer surpasses all men in this quality.

10. Her time was filled by regular occupations.

11. I say this to you wholly in confidence.

Chapter 30: Analysis: Phrases as Modifiers

Sentence Analysis

❧

"Analysis" is a Greek word which means "the act of breaking up." Here is the basic method to use for analyzing sentences:

1. Divide each sentence by drawing a vertical line between the complete subject and the complete predicate.

2. Underline the simple subject once and the simple predicate twice.

3. Mention the modifiers of the subject and label them, whether adjectives or adjective phrases.

4. Mention the modifiers of the predicate and label them, whether adverbs or adverbial phrases.

I.

Analyze the sentences from chapter 29, Exercise III (reprinted below) as follows:
(1) **Divide** each sentence by drawing a vertical line between the complete subject and the complete predicate.
(2) **Underline** the simple subject **once** and the simple predicate **twice**.
(3) **Place** parentheses around adjective and adverbial phrases.
(4) Mention the modifiers of the subject and **label** them with **Adj**, whether adjectives or adjective phrases.
(5) Mention the modifiers of the predicate and **label** them with **Adv**, whether adverbs or adverbial phrases.

1. Early in the morning a sudden storm drove us within two or three leagues of Ireland.

2. These things terrified the people to the last degree.

3. At the first glimpse of dawn he hastened to the prison.

4. The wall fell with a crash.

5. By daybreak we had sailed out of sight of land.

6. The full light of day had now risen upon the desert.

7. With smiles the rising morn we greet.

8. Innumerable dismal stories we heard every day.

9. Homer surpasses all men in this quality.

10. Her time was filled by regular occupations.

11. I say this to you wholly in confidence.

II.
(1) In the following sentences place **parentheses** around all the prepositional phrases and **label** the adjective phrases with **Adj** or adverbial phrases with **Adv**.
(2) **Draw an arrow** to the noun or pronoun which the adjective phrase modifies, or to the verb, adjective, or adverb which the adverbial phrase modifies.

1. A long journey lay before us.

2. The kitchen soon was all on fire.

3. The sea fowl is gone to her nest;

   The beast is laid down in his lair.

4. He was regarded as a merchant of great wealth.

5. The night was Winter in his roughest mood.

6. The chiming clocks to dinner call.

7. The blanket of night is drawn asunder for a moment.

8. Green pastures she views in the midst of the dale.

9. In this state of breathless agitation did I stand for some time.

10. The solution of this difficulty must come from you.

11. Grapevines here and there twine themselves round shrub and tree.

12. Our coach rattled out of the city.

13. La Fleur flew out of the room like lightning.

14. Graham came from his hiding place in the neighboring mountains.

15. Battles and skirmishes were fought on all sides.

16. The stone cannot be moved from its place by any force.

17. In silent horror o'er the boundless waste

    The driver Hassan with his camels passed.

18. They sat them down upon the yellow sand,

    Between the sun and moon upon the shore.

19. Large towns were founded in different parts of the kingdom.

20. My days now rolled on in a perfect dream of happiness.

Chapter 30: Additional Exercises

Practice identifying phrases.
>   (1) **Underline** the noun phrases **once**.
>   (2) **Underline** the verb and verb phrases **twice**.
>   (3) Draw **parentheses** around the adjective phrases and label with **Adj**.
>   (4) Draw **square brackets** around the adverbial phrases and label with **Adv**.

1. The British Parliament and the American Congress are lawmaking bodies.

2. The brave fireman had risked his life.

3. We were attacked on every side.

4. The gates of Amsterdam had been barred against him.

5. Birds of prey were wheeling about.

6. I have received a letter from my aunt.

7. The inn was beset by robbers.

8. The messenger was arrested and searched, and the letters from the enemy were found.

9. The roar of guns and the clang of bells lasted all night.

10. I have come here without an invitation.

11. Tom obeyed against his will.

12. In spite of his efforts the man could not swim against the tide.

13. A huge alligator was sunning himself on the bank.

14. An old dog cannot learn new tricks.

15. Speak in a loud, clear voice.

Chapter 31: Number

I.

In the following extracts **underline** all the plural nouns. **Give the singular** of each.

1. The stranger who would form a correct opinion of the English character must not confine his observations to the metropolis. He must go forth into the country; he must sojourn in villages and hamlets; he must visit castles, villas, farmhouses, villages; he must wander through parks and gardens, along hedges and green lanes; he must loiter about country churches; attend wakes and fairs, and other rural festivals; and cope with the people in all their conditions and all their habits and humors. — Irving.

2. My raft was now strong enough to bear any reasonable weight. My next care was what to load it with, and how to preserve what I laid upon it from the surf of the sea. But I was not long considering this. I first laid all the plank or boards upon it that I could get; and, having considered well what I most wanted, I first got three of the seamen's chests, which I had broken open and emptied, and lowered them down upon my raft. The first of these I filled with provisions, — bread, rice, three Dutch cheeses, five pieces of dried goat's flesh, which we lived much upon, and a little remainder of European corn which had been laid by for some fowls which we brought to sea with us; but the fowls were killed. There had been some barley and wheat together, but, to my great disappointment, I found afterwards that the rats had eaten or spoiled it all. — Defoe.

3. Weavers, nailers, rope makers, artisans of every degree and calling, thronged forward to join the procession from every gloomy and narrow street.

II.

Write a description of some farm, or piece of woods, or town, or village, that you know well.

Label the nouns with **N** and adjectives **Adj**.

Give the plural of every noun that you have used in the singular and the singular of every plural noun.

_____

_____

_____

_____

_____

_____

_____

_____

_____

_____

_____

_____

_____

_____

_____

_____

_____

_____

_____

_____

_____

_____

_____

Chapter 32: Genitive or Possessive Case

Fill each blank with a **genitive** (possessive modifier).

1. The _____ efforts were successful.

2. The _____ life was spared at the request of his comrades.

3. _____ brother lives in Kentucky.

4. The _____ paw was caught in the trap.

5. The _____ rifle went off by accident.

6. The _____ bravery saved the ship with all the passengers.

7. The _____ eyes shone with excitement.

Chapter 33: Forms of the Genitive

I.

Underline all the genitives (possessive modifiers) and **draw an arrow** to the noun or pronoun that it modifies.

1. The emperor's palace is in the center of the city, where the two great streets meet.

2. Oliver's education began when he was about three years old.

3. Caesar scorns the poet's lays.

4. The silver light, with quivering glance,

   Played on the water's still expanse.

5. Here on this beach a hundred years ago,

   Three children of three houses, Annie Lee,

   The prettiest little damsel in the port,

   And Philip Ray, the miller's only son,

   And Enoch Arden, a rough sailor's lad,

   Made orphan by a winter shipwreck, played

   Among the waste and lumber of the shore.

6. It is not the greatness of a man's means that makes him independent, so much as the

   smallness of his wants.

7. In faith and hope the world will disagree,

   But all mankind's concern is charity.

8. The jester's speech made the duke laugh.

9. A man's nature runs either to herbs or weeds.

II.

Write sentences containing the **genitive singular** of each of the following nouns:

boy _____

girl _____

dog_____

cat_____

John _____

Mary _____

Sarah _____

William _____

spider _____

frog _____

elephant _____

captain_____

sailor _____

soldier _____

chieftain _____

Shakespeare _____

Milton _____

Whittier_____

baker _____

manufacturer _____

chimney sweep _____

III.
Write sentences containing the **genitive** of the names of twelve persons whom you know.

1. _____

2. _____

3. _____

4. _____

5. _____

6. _____

7. _____

8. _____

9. _____

10. _____

11. _____

12. _____

IV.

Underline all the genitives and **label** each singular **S** or plural **P** above the genitive. Be prepared to explain your reason.

1. The monarch's wrath began to rise.

2. They err who imagine that this man's courage was ferocity.

3. Two years' travel in distant and barbarous countries has accustomed me to bear privations.

4. Hark! hark! the lark at heaven's gate sings.

5. Portia dressed herself and her maid in men's apparel.

6. He waved his huntsman's cap on high.

7. The Porters' visit was all but over.

8. The ladies' colds kept them at home all the evening.

9. The crags repeat the ravens' croak.

10. Farmer Grove's house is on fire!

11. The Major paced the terrace in front of the house for his two hours' constitutional walk.

V.

Write sentences containing the **genitive** plural of all the common nouns in Exercise II.

boy _____

girl _____

dog_____

cat_____

John _____

Mary _____

Sarah _____

William _____

spider _____

frog _____

elephant _____

captain _____

sailor _____

soldier _____

chieftain _____

Shakespeare _____

Milton _____

Whittier _____

baker _____

manufacturer _____

chimney sweep _____

VI.

Insert the **apostrophe** in the proper place in every word that needs it.

1. The mans hair was black.

2. The mens courage was almost gone.

3. The spiders web was too weak to hold the flies.

4. The whole clan bewailed the warriors death.

5. The soldiers helmets were visible.

6. I gave him a months notice.

7. Six months time had elapsed.

8. Womens wages are lower than mens.

9. A womans wit has saved many a stupid man.

10. The chieftains sons are the most devoted of brothers.

Chapter 34: Genitive of Pronouns (Possessive Pronouns)

The nominative and the genitive (possessive) forms of several important pronouns are shown in the chart below.

NOMINATIVE SINGULAR	GENITIVE SINGULAR	NOMINATIVE PLURAL	GENITIVE PLURAL
I	my *or* mine	we	our *or* ours
thou	thy *or* thine	you *or* ye	your *or* yours
he	his	they	their *or* theirs
she	her *or* hers	they	their *or* theirs
it	its	they	their *or* theirs

Make sentences containing all the forms of pronouns given above.

1. _____

2. _____

3. _____

4. _____

5. _____

6. _____

7. _____

8. _____

9. _____

10. _____

11. _____

12. _____

13. _____

14. _____

15. _____

16. _____

17. _____

18. _____

19. _____

20. _____

Chapter 35: Genitive Replaced by an *Of*-Phrase

I.

Make twenty sentences each containing a **genitive**. Let them express your own thoughts.

1. _____

2. _____

3. _____

4. _____

5. _____

6. _____

7. _____

8. _____

9. _____

10. _____

11. _____

12. _____

13. _____

14. _____

15. _____

16. _____

17. _____

18. _____

19. _____

20. _____

Replace each genitive with an *of*-phrase, and note the effect. Is the change an improvement or not?

1. _____
2. _____
3. _____
4. _____
5. _____
6. _____
7. _____
8. _____
9. _____
10. _____
11. _____
12. _____
13. _____
14. _____
15. _____
16. _____
17. _____
18. _____
19. _____
20. _____

II.

Make sentences containing either the genitive of each of the following nouns or an *of*-phrase replacing the genitive. Tell the grounds of your choice.

1. boy _____
2. girl_____
3. mayor_____
4. boys _____
5. girls_____
6. men_____

7. man _____

8. Chicago _____

9. horse _____

10. horses _____

11. Charles _____

12. Mr. Williams _____

13. Boston _____

14. friendship _____

15. bandit _____

16. pirate _____

17. senator _____

18. Shakespeare _____

19. tree _____

20. Longfellow _____

21. house _____

22. wisdom _____

23. school _____

24. chimney _____

25. grocer _____

26. pansy _____

27. rose _____

28. lesson _____

29. century _____

30. bicycle _____

31. Julius _____

Chapter 36: Analysis: Genitive and *Of*-Phrase

Analyze the sentences below, as follows:

(1) **Divide** each sentence by drawing a vertical line between the complete subject and the complete predicate.
(2) **Underline** the simple subject **once** and the simple predicate **twice**.
(3) **Place** parentheses around adjective and adverbial phrases.
(4) Mention the modifiers of the subject and **label** them with **Adj**, whether adjectives or adjective phrases. Treat the genitives and *of*-phrases as adjective modifiers and **label** them **Adj**.
(5) Mention the modifiers of the predicate and **label** them with **Adv**, whether adverbs or adverbial phrases.

1. The chieftain's brow darkened.

2. Quickly sped the hours of that happy day.

3. Their friends have abandoned them.

4. Edison's great discovery was then announced.

5. The population of Chicago is increasing rapidly.

6. The captain of the steamer stood on the bridge.

7. The men's last hope had vanished.

8. Our distress was soon relieved.

9. The branches of the tree droop gracefully.

10. The bird's song rang out merrily.

11. A huntsman's life had always attracted me.

Chapter 37: Apposition

I.

Fill the blanks with **appositives**.

1. Mr. Jones, the _____ , is building a house for me.

2. Have you seen Rover, my _____, anywhere?

3. Animals of all kinds, _____, _____, _____, and _____, were exhibited in the menagerie.

4. Chapman, the _____ of the team, broke his collar bone.

5. My new kite, _____ from my uncle, is caught in the tree.

6. Washington, the _____ of the United States, is on the Potomac.

7. Who has met my young friend _____ today?

8. Charles I, _____ of England, was beheaded in 1649.

9. Washington, the _____ of his country, was born in 1732.

10. Tiger-hunting, a dangerous _____, was the sultan's chief delight.

II.

Underline the appositives, and **circle** the noun to which each is attached.

1. An Englishwoman, the wife of one of the officers, was sitting on the battlements with her child in her arms.

2. I went to visit Mr. Hobbes, the famous philosopher.

3. We were hopeful boys, all three of us.

4. Spring, the sweet Spring, is the year's pleasant king.

5. Then forth they all out of their baskets drew
   Great store of flowers, the honor of the field.

6. He was speedily summoned to the apartment of his captain, the Lord Crawford.

7. No rude sound shall reach thine ear,
   Armor's clang and war-steed champing.

8. And thus spake on that ancient man,
   The bright-eyed mariner.

9. There lived at no great distance from this stronghold a farmer, a bold and stout man, whose name was Binnock.

Chapter 38: Analysis: The Appositive

I.

Underline the appositives.

1. Stuart, the dauntless explorer, perished in the desert.

2. Spring, the sweet spring, is the year's pleasant king.

3. Quentin's captain, the Lord Crawford, summoned him.

4. The hiss of the serpent, a blood-curdling sound, was heard in the darkness.

5. The old sailor, a weather-beaten Scot, told a strange story.

6. The farmer, a bold, strong man, lived not far from the fort.

7. We, your oldest friends, will help you.

8. The castle, a battered ruin, stood by the river.

9. Ferguson, an earnest patriot, addressed the crowd.

II.

Analyze the sentences in Exercise I, reproduced below.
    (1) **Underline** the complete subject **once.**
    (2) **Underline** the complete predicate **twice.**
    (3) **Label** the simple subject with **S.**
    (4) **Label** the simple predicate with **V.**
    (5) **Label** the appositive noun with **A** and its modifiers with **Adj.**

1. Stuart, the dauntless explorer, perished in the desert.

2. Spring, the sweet spring, is the year's pleasant king.

3. Quentin's captain, the Lord Crawford, summoned him.

4. The hiss of the serpent, a blood-curdling sound, was heard in the darkness.

5. The old sailor, a weather-beaten Scot, told a strange story.

6. The farmer, a bold, strong man, lived not far from the fort.

7. We, your oldest friends, will help you.

8. The castle, a battered ruin, stood by the river.

9. Ferguson, an earnest patriot, addressed the crowd.

Chapter 39: Transitive and Intransitive Verbs — The Direct Object

I.

Underline the verbs and verb phrases in the following passages. **Label** the transitive verbs with a **T** and the intransitive verbs with an **I**. **Label** the direct objects with **DO**.

1. A small party of the musketeers followed me.

2. These, therefore, I can pity.

3. Through the darkness and the cold we flew.

4. Yet I insisted, yet you answered not.

5. The enemy made frequent and desperate sallies.

6. Fierce passions discompose the mind.

7. The gallant greyhounds swiftly ran.

8. The Scots killed the cattle of the English.

9. Down the ashes shower like rain.

10. While Spain built up her empire in the New World, the English seamen reaped a humbler

   harvest in the fisheries of New-Foundland.

II.

In several pronouns the objective case has a special form, different from that of the nominative. Thus,

> *I* have a knife.   *He* is my friend.
> You blame *me*.   I like *him*.

Fill in the blanks with **pronouns** in the **objective** case.

1. They found _____ in the woods.

2. My friend asked _____ to dinner.

3. The savage dog bit _____ severely.

4. Our teacher has sent _____ home.

5. Their uncle visited _____ last week.

6. The rain drenched _____ in spite of my umbrella.

7. Mary's brother helped_____ with her lesson.

8. Arthur's book interests _____ very much.

9. The flood drove _____ from our farm.

10. A boat carried _____ across the river.

Chapter 40: Analysis: The Direct Object

I.

Analyze the following sentences

(1) **Write** in the blank whether the sentence is declarative with **D**, interrogative with **Int**, imperative with **Imp**, or exclamatory with **E**.

(2) **Underline** the complete subject **once** and **underline** the complete predicate **twice**.

(3) **Label** the simple subject with **S** and the simple predicate with **V**.

(4) **Label** adjective modifiers with **Adj.**

(5) **Label** the adverb modifiers with **Adv.**

(6) **Label** the direct object with **DO** and the transitive verb with **T**.

1. _____Jane wrote a hurried note.

2. _____The baron pardoned the young couple.

3. _____Every science has its undiscovered mysteries.

4. _____We heard the sound of music in the distance.

5. _____He turned away and strode off in the opposite direction.

6. _____The sheep and the cow have no cutting teeth in the upper jaw.

7. _____A tap on her door interrupted these musings.

8. _____Bessy's lip trembled and the color sprang to her face.

9. _____How had the gentle spirit of that good man sweetened our natures!

II.

Analyze the following sentences as you did in Exercise I.

1. _____How I envied the happy groups on the tops of the stagecoaches!

2. _____The carriage came on at a furious rate.

3. _____The Highlanders suddenly flung away their muskets, drew their broadswords, and

      rushed forward with a fearful yell.

4. _____I see the path of duty before me.

5. _____Nothing could resist their onset.

6. _____The fleet bombarded the town.

7. _____A crowd of children was following the piper about the streets.

8. _____Streams of lava rolled down the side of the mountain.

9. _____The anchor would not hold the ship.

10. _____The bomb exploded and scattered destruction.

11. _____The tide ebbed and left the boat on the bar.

12. _____A terrible earthquake has almost destroyed the city.

13. _____The flames poured out of the upper windows of the factory.

14. _____The conspirators attacked Caesar in the Senate-house. He resisted them for a time,

      but at last fell at the foot of Pompey's statue.

Chapter 41: Active and Passive Voice

I.

Underline the passive verbs and verb phrases. **Label** the subject of each sentence with an **S.**

1. My command was promptly obeyed.

2. One of the men who robbed me was taken.

3. Now were the gates of the city broken down by General Monk.

4. Suddenly, while I gazed, the loud crash of a thousand cymbals was heard.

5. Judgment is forced upon us by experience.

6. Nature is often hidden, sometimes overcome, seldom extinguished.

7. Youth is always delighted with applause.

8. The hall was immediately cleared by the soldiery.

9. Just before midnight the castle was blown up.

10. My spirits were raised by the rapid motion of the journey.

11. A great council of war was held in the king's quarters.

12. Many consciences were awakened; many hard hearts were melted into tears; many a

    penitent confession was made.

II.

Change each verb from the active form to the passive.
Note that the object will become the subject.

      Example: Her friends loved *her.*
                            She was loved by her friends.

1. The sailor rescued the child.

_____

2. Columbus discovered America.

_____

3. The French settled Louisiana.

_____

4. Intemperance wrecked the man's life.

_____

5. Edward VII succeeded Victoria.

_____

6. The Americans captured Major André.

_____

7. Longfellow wrote "Hiawatha."

_____

8. Robert Fulton invented the steamboat.

_____

9. Exercises in analysis sharpen our wits.

_____

10. An eclipse of the sun terrified the savages.

_____

11. Julius Caesar twice invaded Britain.

_____

12. Tom's clever play won the game.

_____

13. A landslide buried the house.

_____

14. Lightning struck the statue.

_____

15. Her brother's unkindness grieved Jane.

_____

Chapter 42: Predicate Adjective

Circle the predicate adjectives. **Underline** the subject of the sentence which is described by the predicate adjective.

1. The river was now full of life and motion.

2. The sentiments of the hearers were various.

3. In the north the storm grew thick.

4. Soon his eyes grew brilliant.

5. Some fortifications still remained entire.

6. He lay prostrate on the ground.

7. The evening proved fine.

8. Alfred Burnham has become penitent.

9. How different the place looked now!

10. She seemed anxious to get away without speaking.

11. Their hearts are grown desperate.

12. The captain appeared impatient.

13. He began to look a little less stern and terrible.

14. Many houses were then left desolate.

15. Gertrude remained aghast and motionless.

16. He stood stubborn and rigid.

17. All my efforts were in vain.

18. These threats sounded alarming.

19. The same law holds good.

20. She seemed anxious and looked pale.

21. Such conduct is thought improper.

22. The air was fresh but balmy.

23. He lay for a long while motionless and silent.

24. A great part of the island is rather level.

25. Their conversation was gay and animated.

26. He had become sluggish and self-indulgent.

27. Martha was blunt and plain-spoken to a fault.

28. In the tall towers by the wayside the bells hung mute.

29. Lochiel was wise in council, eloquent in debate, ready in devising expedients, and skillful in managing the minds of men.

30. Captain Brown and Miss Jenkyns were not very cordial to each other.

II.
Fill in each blank with a **predicate adjective**. Observe that each adjective completes the predicate but describes the subject.

1. The storm came on very suddenly. The whole landscape became _____.

2. The lake is _____ today.

3. Seals look _____, but are not dangerous.

4. The dog proved _____ to his master.

5. Washington was _____ in war and _____ in peace.

6. The leaves turn _____ in the autumn.

7. John has grown very _____ in the past year.

8. Every lesson seems _____ to the indolent.

9. Such conduct appears _____ to me.

10. Do not look so _____.

11. Why does Mary seem so _____?

12. Is the ice _____? It looks _____ enough.

13. You do not appear very _____.

14. The iron grew _____ in the fire.

15. Your affection for you friend has grown _____.

16. The weather has been _____ of late.

17. Be _____, and you will be _____.

18. Never be _____, for carelessness is stupidity.

Chapter 43: Predicate Nominative

I.

Make seven sentences containing a predicate nominative after *am, is, are, was, were, has been, or had been*. Select the subjects of your sentences from the following list:

Thomas Jefferson, Columbus, elms, ash, carriage, sword, story, scissors, history, pencil, ships, Carlo, football, oranges, peace, lemons, war, kindness, verb, noun, pronoun.

1. am _____

2. is_____

3. are _____

4. was_____

5. were_____

6. has been _____

7. had been _____

II.

Fill in each blank with a predicate nominative.

1. Thomas Smith is my _____.

2. My father's name is _____.

3. A noun is the _____ of a person, place, or thing.

4. A pronoun is a _____ used instead of a noun.

5. The banana is a delicious _____.

6. The boys are all _____.

7. Napoleon was _____ of France.

8. Albert has been your _____ for many years.

9. We had been _____ in England.

10. My birthday present will be a _____.

11. Fire is a good _____ but a bad _____.

12. Hunger is the best _____.

13. Our five senses are _____, _____, _____, _____,

and _____.

14. My favorite flower has always been the_____.

15. A friend in need is a _____ indeed.

16. Virtue is its own _____.

17. My favorite game is _____.

18. Milton was an English _____.

19. "Hiawatha" is a _____ by Longfellow.

20. Benjamin Franklin was a _____.

21. John Adams was the second _____ of the United States.

Chapter 44: Direct Object and Predicate Nominative Distinguished

I.

Underline the subjects **once** and the simple predicates **twice**. **Label** the predicate nominatives with **PN**.

1. He is an honest man and an honest writer.

2. The Malay has been a fearful enemy for months.

3. King Malcolm was a brave and wise prince.

4. You had been the great instrument of preserving your country from foreign and domestic ruin.

5. Still he continued an incorrigible rascal.

6. Dewdrops are the gems of morning,

   But the tears of mournful eve.

7. While still very young, she became the wife of a Greek adventurer.

8. Every instant now seemed an age.

9. Dr. Daniel Dove was a perfect doctor, and his horse Nobs was a perfect horse.

10. Francis the First stood before my mind the abstract and model of perfection and greatness.

11. The name of Francis Drake became the terror of the Spanish Indies.

12. Great barkers are no biters.

13. I hope she will prove a well-disposed girl.

14. He may prove a troublesome appendage to us.

15. His bridge was only loose planks laid upon large trestles.

16. I entered the town a candle-snuffer, and I quitted it a hero!

17. A very complaisant and agreeable companion may, and often does, prove a very improper and a very dangerous friend.

18. Real friendship is a slow grower.

19. He became a friend of Mrs. Wilberforce's.

20. My friends fall around me, and I shall be left a lonely tree before I am withered.

II.
Label the predicate nominatives with **PN** and the direct objects with **DO.**

1. With how sad steps, O Moon, thou climb'st the sky!

2. The landscape was a forest wide and bare.

3. Here the Albanian proudly treads the ground.

4. Wing thy flight from hence on the morrow.

5. It was a wild and strange retreat

    As e'er was trod by outlaw's feet.

6. Honor is the subject of my story.

7. I alone became their prisoner.

8. A strange group we were.

9. The mountain mist took form and limb

    Of noontide hag or goblin grim.

10. The family specialties were health, good-humor, and vivacity.

11. The deep war-drum's sound announced the close of day.

12. You seem a sober ancient gentleman.

13. His house, his home, his heritage, his lands,

    He left without a sigh.

14. On the tenth day of June, 1703, a boy on the topmast discovered land.

15. Have you turned coward?

16. This goodly frame, the earth, seems to me a sterile promontory.

17. This southern tempest soon

    May change its quarter with the changing moon.

18. Mr. Bletson arose and paid his respects to Colonel Everard.

19. Escape seemed a desperate and impossible adventure.

20. Here I reign king.

21. She uttered a half-stifled shriek.

22. The sailors joined his prayer in silent thought.

23. We have been lamenting your absence.

24. This spark will prove a raging fire.

Chapter 45: Pronoun as Predicate Nominative

Errors in the use of pronouns are common.

The pronouns in the following sentences are correctly used. **Label** the subjects with **S** and the predicate nominatives with **PN**.

1. "Who's there?" "It's I!"

2. I wish to see Mr. Smith. Are you he?

3. "Do you know John Anson? "Yes, that's he!"

4. See that poor fellow! I shouldn't like to be he.

5. I asked to see your sons. Are these they?"

   "Yes, these are they. Shall I tell you their names?"

6. "It's she! There she is!" cried the children eagerly.

7. Yes, it was he, — the famous admiral.

8. I wish it hadn't been I that broke the window.

9. If that is the rich Mrs. Blank, I shouldn't like to be she.

10. "Who's there?" "It's we." "Who are you?"

11. The best grammarians in the village are we four girls.

Chapter 46: Analysis: Predicate Nominative and Predicate Adjective

Analyze sentences from chapter 44, Exercise II, 1-4, 6-15 in accordance with the plan below. Although sentences 5 and 16-24 are not assigned, they are included here for optional extra practice.

(1) **Divide** each sentence into the complete subject and the complete predicate with a **vertical line**.

(2) **Underline** the simple subject **once** and the predicate **twice**.

(3) **Place** parentheses around the phrases.

(4) **Label** the modifiers of the subject and of the predicate, adjectives with **Adj**, adverbs with **Adv**.

(5) **Label** the direct object with **DO**, the predicate nominative with **PN**, or the predicate adjective with **PA**, if the sentence has any of these parts.

(6) **Label** the modifiers of the direct object, etc. with **Adj** or **Adv.**

1. With how sad steps, O Moon, thou climb'st the sky!

2. The landscape was a forest wide and bare.

3. Here the Albanian proudly treads the ground.

4. Wing thy flight from hence on the morrow.

5. It was a wild and strange retreat

   As e'er was trod by outlaw's feet.

6. Honor is the subject of my story.

7. I alone became their prisoner.

8. A strange group we were.

9. The mountain mist took form and limb

   Of noontide hag or goblin grim.

10. The family specialties were health, good humor, and vivacity.

11. The deep war-drum's sound announced the close of day.

12. You seem a sober ancient gentleman.

13. His house, his home, his heritage, his lands,

    He left without a sigh.

14. On the tenth day of June, 1703, a boy on the topmast discovered land.

15. Have you turned coward?

16. This goodly frame, the earth, seems to me a sterile promontory.

17. This southern tempest soon

    May change its quarter with the changing moon.

18. Mr. Bletson arose and paid his respects to Colonel Everard.

19. Escape seemed a desperate and impossible adventure.

20. Here I reign king.

21. She uttered a half-stifled shriek.

22. The sailors joined his prayer in silent thought.

23. We have been lamenting your absence.

24. This spark will prove a raging fire.

Chapter 47: Simple Subject and Compound Subject

I.

Use the following substantives, in pairs, joined by conjunctions, as the compound subjects of sentences:

Europe, Asia _____

boots, shoes _____

wood, iron _____

justice, mercy _____

fire, sword _____

goodness, truth _____

masons, carpenters _____

apples, oranges _____

books, pencil _____

father, mother _____

gulfs, bays _____

hills, plains _____

maple, cedar_____

thunder, lightning_____

II.

Divide the following sentences with a vertical line into their complete subjects and complete predicates.

Underline the several substantives that make up each compound subject, and **circle** the conjunctions that join them.

1. Sorrow and sadness sat upon every face.

2. These terrors and apprehensions of the people led them into a thousand weak, foolish, and wicked things.

3. Tears lie in him, and consuming fire.

4. Homer and Socrates and the Christian apostles belong to old days.

5. My childish years and his hasty departure prevented me from enjoying the full benefit of his lessons.

6. Everywhere new pleasures, new interests awaited me.

7. His integrity and benevolence are equal to his learning.

8. Both saw and axe were plied vigorously.

9. Neither Turk nor Tartar can frighten him.

10. The duke and his senators left the court.

11. Either Rome or Carthage must perish.

12. Her varying color, her clouded brow, her thoughtful yet wandering eye, so different from the usual open, bland expression of her countenance, plainly indicated the state of her feelings.

13. Moss and clay and leaves combined

    To fence each crevice from the wind.

14. Tower and town and cottage

    Have heard the trumpet's blast.

15. The horsemen and the footmen

    Are pouring in amain

    From many a stately marketplace,

    From many a fruitful plain.

16. Groans and shrieks filled the air.

17. The walls and gates of the town were strongly guarded.

18. Chariots, horses, men, were huddled together.

Chapter 48: Simple Predicate and Compound Predicate

I.

Divide the sentences with a vertical line into their complete subjects and complete predicates. **Underline** each verb or verb phrase that make up each compound predicate and **circle** the conjunction that joins them.

1. The wakeful bloodhound rose, and shook his hide.

2. They clambered through the cavity, and began to go down on the other side.

3. During this time, I neither saw nor heard of Alethe.

4. The blackbird amid leafy trees,

   The lark above the hill,

   Let loose their carols when they please,

   Are quiet when they will.

5. She immediately scrambled across the fence and walked away.

6. John made no further reply, but left the room sullenly, whistling as he went.

7. I dressed myself, took my hat and gloves, and lingered a little in the room.

8. The sun had just risen and, from the summit of the Arabian hills, was pouring down his beams into that vast valley of waters.

9. They kept up the Christmas carol, sent true-love knots on Valentine morning, ate pancakes on Shrovetide, showed their wit on the first of April, and religiously cracked nuts on Michaelmas eve.

II.

Use the following verbs and verb phrases in pairs to make the compound predicate of sentences:

seek, find _____

rose, spoke_____

wrote, sent_____

has fished, has caught _____

heard, told _____

tries, fails _____

Chapter 48: Review Exercises

I.

Review chapter 25, Exercises II and III, and observe the compound subjects and predicates that you made. List them here.

<u>Exercise II</u>

List the compound subjects or predicates (remember that adverbs or adjectives connected by a conjunction are not compound subjects or predicates).

1. _____

2. _____

3. _____

4. _____

5. _____

6. _____

7. _____

8. _____

9. _____

10. _____

11. _____

12. _____

13. _____

14. _____

15. _____

16. _____

17. _____

18. _____

19. _____

20. _____

21. _____

22. _____

23. _____

Exercise III

List the compound subjects or predicates (be careful not to include compound *sentences* that were formed with conjunctions).

1. _____

2. _____

3. _____

4. _____

5. _____

6. _____

7. _____

8. _____

9. _____

10. _____

11. _____

II.
Analyze the following sentences:

 (1) **Divide** each sentence into the complete subject and the complete predicate with a **vertical line**.

 (2) **Underline** the simple subject **once** and the predicate **twice**.

 (3) **Place** parentheses around the phrases.

 (4) **Label** the modifiers of the subject and of the predicate, adjectives with **Adj**, adverbs with **Adv**.

 (5) **Label** the direct object with **DO**, the predicate nominative with **PN**, the predicate adjective with **PA**, and conjunctions with **C**, if the sentence has any of these parts.

 (6) **Label** the modifiers of the direct object, etc. with **Adj** or **Adv.**

1. The wind was either too light or blew from the wrong quarter.

2. They obey their guide, and are happy.

3. The stranger neither spoke nor read English.

4. The water looked muddy and tasted brackish, but was eagerly drunk by the travelers.

5. The watchman was sleepy, but struggled against his drowsiness.

6. The fox was caught, but escaped.

7. The bear growled fiercely, but did not touch the boy.

8. The sails were drying, and flapped lazily against the mast.

9. The ladies and gentlemen were inclined to sneer, and were giggling audibly.

10. From the first, Miss Rice was interested in her servant, and encouraged her confidences.

11. He jumped into the gondola and was carried away through the silence of the night.

12. She grew pale herself and dropped his hand suddenly.

13. Reuben came in hurriedly and nodded a goodbye to all of us.

14. Gravely he greets each city sire,

 Commends each pageant's quaint attire,

Gives to the dancers thanks aloud,

And smiles and nods upon the crowd.

15. Flesh and blood could not endure such hardships.

Chapter 49: Clauses — Compound Sentences

Separate these compound sentences into the clauses of which they are composed. **Draw brackets** around the clause. **Underline** any the conjunctions that connect the clauses.

1. The door opened, and the two men came out.

2. They seemed mere machines, and all their thoughts were employed in the care of their horses.

3. The neighbors stared and sighed, yet they blessed the lad.

4. Thy heart is sad, thy home is far away.

5. Days and weeks slide imperceptibly away; November is just at hand, and the half of it will soon be over.

6. Pass beneath the archway into the court, and the sixteenth century closes around you.

7. The ocean has its ebbings—so has grief.

8. Art thou here, or is it but a dream?

9. The robins are not good solo singers, but their chorus is unrivaled.

10. Summer was now coming on with hasty steps, and my seventeenth birthday was fast approaching.

11. The night had been heavy and lowering, but towards the morning it had changed to a slight frost, and the ground and the trees were now covered with rime.

12. The war-pipes ceased, but lake and hill

    Were busy with their echoes still.

13. St. Agnes' Eve — ah, bitter chill it was!

    The owl, for all his feathers, was a-cold;

    The hare limped trembling through the frozen grass,

    And silent was the flock in woolly fold.

Chapter 50: Complex Sentences — Adverbial Clauses

I.

Separate each complex sentence into the main and the subordinate clause. **Underline** the main clause **once** and the subordinate clause **twice**.

Label the adverbs with **Adv** or conjunctions with **C** that connect the clauses. (See Sections 199 and 200 for a list of these words.)

1. King Robert was silent when he heard this story.

2. He laughed till the tears ran down his face.

3. When the Arabs saw themselves out of danger, they slackened their pace.

4. We advance in freedom as we advance in years.

5. When I came back I resolved to settle in London.

6. As he approached the stream, his heart began to thump.

7. He struggled on, though he was very tired.

8. I consent because you wish it.

9. Dr. Acton came down while I was there.

10. We drove along through a beautiful country till at length we came to the brow of a steep hill.

11. As we grow old, our sense of the value of time becomes vivid.

12. Just when the oak leaves first looked reddish, the whole tribe of finches burst forth in songs from every bough.

13. Jason and the bull wrestled until the monster fell groveling on his knees.

14. If any dispute arises, they apply to him for the decision.

15. If this is no violent exercise, I am much mistaken.

16. Tell me the facts, since you know them.

II.

Analyze the sentences in Exercise I, reproduced on the following page. Identify the following elements:

    (1) **Underline** complete subject **once** and complete predicate **twice**.
    (2) **Label** simple subject with **S** and simple predicate with **V.**
    (3) **Place** parentheses around phrases and brackets around clauses.
    (4) **Label** modifiers (adverbs with **Adv**, adjectives with **Adj**, adverbial clauses with **Adv.**)

(5) **Analyze** the subordinate clause (**label** the subject with **S**, verb or verb phrase with **V** and modifiers with **Adj/** or **Adv**).

1. King Robert was silent when he heard this story.

2. He laughed till the tears ran down his face.

3. When the Arabs saw themselves out of danger, they slackened their pace.

4. We advance in freedom as we advance in years.

5. When I came back I resolved to settle in London.

6. As he approached the stream, his heart began to thump.

7. He struggled on, though he was very tired.

8. I consent because you wish it.

9. Dr. Acton came down while I was there.

10. We drove along through a beautiful country till at length we came to the brow of a steep hill.

11. As we grow old, our sense of the value of time becomes vivid.

12. Just when the oak leaves first looked reddish, the whole tribe of finches burst forth in songs from every bough.

13. Jason and the bull wrestled until the monster fell groveling on his knees.

14. If any dispute arises, they apply to him for the decision.

15. If this is no violent exercise, I am much mistaken.

16. Tell me the facts, since you know them.

Chapter 51: Relative Pronouns

I.

Separate each sentence into the main and the subordinate clause by **underlining** the main clause **once** and the subordinate clause **twice**.

Label the subject with **S** and the predicate with **V** of each clause.

1. Harry has lost a knife *which* belongs to me.

2. I have a friend *whose* name is Arthur.

3. The girl *whom* you saw is my sister.

4. Tell me the news *that* you have heard.

In the sentences above the relative pronoun is sometimes a subject, sometimes an object, and once a genitive. Write the case of each relative pronoun in the sentences above on the lines below:

1. _____

2. _____

3. _____

4. _____

II.

Fill in each blank with a **relative pronoun**, and **circle** its **antecedent.**

1. The house _____ stands yonder belongs to Colonel Carton.

2. Are you the man _____ saved my daughter from drowning?

3. The sailor's wife gazed at the stately ship _____ was taking her husband away from her.

4. A young farmer, _____ name was Judkins, was the first to enlist.

5. Nothing _____ you can do will help me.

6. The horses _____ belong to the squire are famous trotters.

7. James Adams is the strongest man _____ I have ever seen.

8. My friend, _____ we had overtaken on his way down town, greeted us cheerfully.

9. Behold the man _____ the king delighteth to honor!

10. That is the captain _____ ship was wrecked last December.

III.
Circle each relative pronoun in the following sentences, and **draw an arrow** to its antecedent.

Underline the main clause **once** and the subordinate clause **twice**. **Label** the subject with **S** and predicate with **V** of each.

1. A sharp rattle was heard on the window, which made the children jump.

2. The small torch that he held sent forth a radiance by which suddenly the whole surface of the desert was illuminated.

3. He that has most time has none to lose.

4. Gray rocks peeped from amidst the lichens and creeping plants which covered them as with a garment of many colors.

5. The enclosed fields, which were generally forty feet square, resembled so many beds of flowers.

6. They that reverence too much old times are but a scorn to the new.

7. The morning came which was to launch me into the world, and from which my whole succeeding life has, in many important points, taken its coloring.

8. Ten guineas, added to about two which I had remaining from my pocket money, seemed to me sufficient for an indefinite length of time.

9. He is the freeman whom the truth makes free.

10. There was one philosopher who chose to live in a tub.

11. Conquerors are a class of men with whom, for the most part, the world could well dispense.

12. The light came from a lamp that burned brightly on the table.

13. The sluggish stream through which we moved yielded sullenly to the oar.

14. The place from which the light proceeded was a small chapel.

15. The warriors went into battle clad in complete armor, which covered them from top to toe.

16. She seemed as happy as a wave

    That dances on the sea.

17. He sang out a long, loud, and canorous peal of laughter, that might have wakened the

    Seven Sleepers.

18. Thou hadst a voice whose sound was like the sea.

19. Many of Douglas's followers were slain in the battle in which he himself fell.

Chapter 52: Adjective Clauses

I.

Underline the adjective clauses.
Circle the substantive (noun or pronoun) that each describes or limits.

1. The careless messenger lost the letter which had been entrusted to him.

2. The merchant gave the sailor who rescued him a thousand dollars.

3. The officer selected seven men, veterans whose courage had often been tested.

4. My traveling companion was an old gentleman whom I had met in Paris.

5. The castle where I was born lies in ruins.

6. Alas! the spring which had watered this oasis was dried up.

7. The time that you have wasted would have made an industrious man rich.

8. A strange fish, which had wings, was this day captured by the seamen.

9. This happened at a time when prices were high.

II.

Analyze the sentences from Exercise I, reproduced below.
    (1) **Underline** complete subject **once** and complete predicate **twice**.
    (2) **Label** simple subject with **S** and simple predicate with **V.**
    (3) **Place** parentheses around phrases and brackets around clauses.
    (4) **Label** modifiers (adverbs with **Adv**, adjectives with **Adj**, adjective clauses with **Adj**).
    (5) Analyze the clauses and **label** the subject with **S,** verb or verb phrase with **V,** and modifiers with **Adj** or **Adv.**

1. The careless messenger lost the letter which had been entrusted to him.

2. The merchant gave the sailor who rescued him a thousand dollars.

3. The officer selected seven men, veterans whose courage had often been tested.

4. My traveling companion was an old gentleman whom I had met in Paris.

5. The castle where I was born lies in ruins.

6. Alas! the spring which had watered this oasis was dried up.

7. The time that you have wasted would have made an industrious man rich.

8. A strange fish, which had wings, was this day captured by the seamen.

9. This happened at a time when prices were high.

Chapter 53: Noun Clauses

I.
Write two sentences showing the use of nouns in each of the following situations:

  a) as subjects
  b) direct objects

  c) predicate nominatives
  d) and appositives

1. _____

2. _____

3. _____

4. _____

5. _____

6. _____

7. _____

8. _____

II.
Underline the noun clauses. If the clause is a subject **label** it with **S**, direct object with **DO**, predicate nominative with **PN**, or appositive with **App**.

1. That some mistake had occurred was evident.

2. That republics are ungrateful is a common saying.

3. That fire burns is one of the first lessons of childhood.

4. That the fever was spreading became only too apparent.

5. I know that he has received a letter.

6. I wish that you would study harder.

7. From that moment I resolved that I would stay in the town.

8. Bassanio confessed to Portia that he had no fortune.

9. My opinion is that this story is false.

10. His decision was that the castle should be surrendered.

11. The saying that the third time never fails is old.

12. The lesson that work is necessary is learned early.

III.

In the following sentences:

    a) **Write** in the blank whether each sentence is **compound** or **complex**.

    b) **Draw** brackets around its clauses.

    c) **Label** the clauses (adjective with **Adj**, adverbial with **Adv**, and noun clauses with **N**).

1. _____All the birds began to sing when the sun rose.

2. _____The house stands where three roads meet.

3. _____He worked hard all his life that he might enjoy leisure in his old age.

4. _____The earth caved in upon the miner so that he was completely buried.

5. _____I will give you ten cents if you will hold my horse.

6. _____The wanderer trudged on, though he was very tired.

7. _____The only obstacle to our sailing was that we had not yet completed our complement of men.

8. _____Spring had come again, after a long, wet winter, and every orchard hollow blushed once more with apple blossoms.

9. _____A great stone that I happened to find by the seashore served me for an anchor.

10. _____If you will go over, I will follow you.

11. _____He would give the most unpalatable advice, if need were.

12. _____The first thing that made its appearance was an enormous ham.

13. _____As Pen followed his companion up the creaking old stair, his knees trembled under him.

14. _____Two old ladies in black came out of the old-fashioned garden; they walked towards a seat and sat down in the autumn landscape.

15. _____The brigand drew a stiletto and rushed upon his adversary. The man eluded the blow and defended himself with his pistol, which had a spring bayonet.

16. _____In the midst of this strait, and hard by a group of rocks called the Hen and Chickens, there lay the wreck of a vessel which had been entangled in the whirlpools and stranded during a storm.

Chapter 54: The Same Word as Different Parts of Speech

I.

Write on the blank whether each of the italicized words is a noun or a verb. Give your reasons.

1. We sit in the warm shade and feel right well
    How the sap creeps up and the blossoms *swell*.

    _____

2. Like the *swell* of some sweet tune
    Morning rises into noon,
    May glides onward into June.

    _____

3. Use your chances while they *last*.

    _____

4. Shoemaker, stick to your *last*.

    _____

5. Down came squirrel, eager for his fare,
    Down came bonny blackbird, I declare!
    Little Bell gave each his honest *share*.

    _____

6. Not what we give, but what we *share*,
    For the gift without the giver is bare.

    _____

7. Heaped in the hollows of the grove, the autumn leaves lie dead,
    They rustle to the eddying gust and to the rabbit's *tread*.

    _____

8. All that *tread* the globe
    Are but a handful to the tribes
    That slumber in its bosom.

    _____

9. But what shall I gain by young Arthur's *fall*?

    _____

10. The woods decay, the woods decay and *fall*.

_____

II.

Use these words in sentences:

    (1) as nouns

    (2) as verbs

1. walk _____

_____

2. use _____

_____

3. order _____

_____

4. alarm _____

_____

5. match _____

_____

6. fish _____

_____

7. fall _____

_____

8. fire _____

_____

9. light _____

_____

10. taste _____

_____

11. faint _____

_____

12. pity _____

_____

13. row _____

_____

14. crowd _____

_____

15. wrong _____

_____

16. rest _____

_____

17. plant _____

_____

18. reply _____

_____

19. ink _____

_____

20. frame _____

_____

21. frown _____

_____

22. dawn _____

_____

23. studies _____

_____

24. pastures _____

_____

25. comforts _____

_____

26. struggles _____

_____

Chapter 55: Nouns and Adjectives

I.

Label each of the italicized words, nouns with **N** or adjectives with **Adj**. Give your reasons.

1. God gives sleep to the *bad* in order that the *good* may be undisturbed.

_____

2. Is thy news *good* or *bad*?

_____

3. She shall be a high and *mighty* queen.

_____

4. He hath put down the *mighty* from their seats.

_____

5. Alexander was a *mighty* conqueror.

_____

6. Give us some *gold*, good Timon! Hast thou more?

_____

7. Man wants but *little* here below,

   "Nor wants that *little* long."

_____

8. The fairy wore a *little* red cap.

_____

9. I heard thee murmur tales of *iron* wars.

_____

10. Strike now, or else the *iron* cools.

_____

11. Without haste, without rest.

    Lifting *better* up to *best*.

_____

12. You are a *better* scholar than I.

_____

13. I stand before you a *free* man.

_____

14. The Star Spangled Banner, O long may it wave

O'er the land of the *free* and the home of the *brave*!

_____

15. Nature ne'er deserts the *wise* and *pure*.

_____

II.
Make sentences of your own, using each of the words studied above:
   (1) as a noun
   (2) as an adjective

1. bad _____

_____

2. good _____

_____

3. mighty _____

_____

4. gold_____

_____

5. little_____

_____

6. iron _____

_____

7. better _____

_____

8. best_____

_____

9. free _____

_____

10. brave _____

_____

11. wise _____

_____

12. pure _____

_____

III.

Make sentences, using each of the following words:
    (1) as a noun
    (2) as an adjective

1. silver _____

_____

2. copper _____

_____

3. wood _____

_____

4. crystal _____

_____

5. leather _____

_____

6. tin _____

_____

7. bold _____

_____

8. cruel _____

_____

9. savage _____

_____

10. generous_____

_____

11. evil _____

_____

12. right _____

_____

13. wrong_____

_____

14. studious _____

_____

15. inexperienced _____

_____

16. young_____

_____

Chapter 56: Adjectives and Adverbs

Study the italicized words and **write** its part of speech (**noun, adjective, adverb**, or **preposition**) in the blank. Remember that the sense determines its usage.

1. _____I must reach town *before* night.

2. _____I have met you *before*.

3. _____Is there anybody *within*?

4. _____*Within* this half hour will he be asleep.

5. _____The city stands on a hill *above* the harbor.

6. _____The sun shines *above*; the waves are dancing.

7. _____He went *by* the house at a great pace.

8. _____He passed *by* on the other side.

9. _____The horse was running *down* the road.

10. _____The lion lay *down* in his lair.

11. _____Come *quick*! We need your help at once.

12. _____Elton was a *quick* and skillful workman.

13. _____This remark cuts me to the *quick*.

14. _____*Hard* work cannot harm a healthy man.

15. _____A healthy man can work *hard*.

16. _____Jack rose *early*, for he meant to go a-fishing.

Chapter 57: Review: Structure of Sentences

There are no written exercises for this chapter.

Chapter 58: Form of Analysis

There are no written exercises for this chapter.

Chapter 59: Inflection

There are no written exercises for this chapter.

Chapter 60: Summary of Inflections

There are no written exercises for this chapter.

Chapter 61: Gender

I.

In the following sentences:

    (1) **Circle** all the pronouns.

    (2) **Label** the gender of each (masculine with **M,** feminine with **F,** or neuter with **N;** if masculine or feminine, such as *their*, use **M/F**).

    (3) **Draw an arrow** to the noun to which each refers.

1. The horse was injured in one of his hind legs.

2. Esther was going to see if she could get some fresh eggs for her mistress's breakfast before the shops closed.

3. All speech, even the commonest speech, has something of song in it.

4. Sam ran out to hold his father's horse.

5. "Now, Doctor," cried the boys, "do tell us your adventures!"

6. Our English archers bent their bows,

   Their hearts were good and true,

   At the first flight of arrows sent,

   Full fourscore Scots they slew.

7. The bridegroom stood dangling his bonnet and plume.

8. Emma was sitting in the midst of the children, telling them a story; and she came smiling towards Erne, holding out her hand.

II.

Fill in each blank with a noun or a pronoun. Tell its **gender**, and give your reason.

1. The poet had written _____ last song.

2. _____ swept the hearth and mended the fire.

3. The old farmer sat in _____ armchair.

4. Tom lost _____ knife; but Philip found _____.

145

5. Arthur and Kate studied _____ lessons together.

6. The Indian picked up a stone and threw _____ at the bird.

7. The tracks were so faint that _____ could not be followed.

8. My aunt has sold _____ horse to _____ cousin.

Chapter 62: Special Rules of Gender, Part 1: Personification

Find examples of personification in a major work of literature from the 19th century. An excerpt from *Two Years Before the Mast* is given for your convenience. **Circle** the pronouns that personify an object.

This day the sun rose clear; we had a fine wind, and everything was bright and cheerful. I had now got my sea legs on, and was beginning to enter upon the regular duties of a sea life. About six bells, that is, three o'clock P.M., we saw a sail on our larboard bow. I was very desirous, like every new sailor, to speak to her. She came down to us, backed her main topsail, and the two vessels stood "head on," bowing and curveting at each other like a couple of war horses reined in by their riders. It was the first vessel that I had seen near, and I was surprised to find how much she rolled and pitched in so quiet a sea. She plunged her head into the sea, and then, her stern settling gradually down, her huge bows rose up, showing the bright copper, and her stern and breasthooks dripping, like old Neptune's locks, with the brine. Her decks were filled with passengers, who had come up at the cry of "Sail ho!" and who, by their dress and features, appeared to be Swiss and French emigrants. She hailed us at first in French, but receiving no answer, she tried us in English. She was the ship *La Carolina*, from Havre, for New York. We desired her to report the brig *Pilgrim*, from Boston, for the northwest coast of America, five days out. She then filled away and left us to plow on through our waste of waters. -RICHARD HENRY DANA, JR.

Why are some objects and qualities regarded as masculine and others as feminine?

_____

_____

_____

Chapter 63: Special Rules of Gender, Part 2: Pronoun for Animals

Write sentences illustrating the gender of nouns and pronouns as follows:

1. Use *he, she,* and *it* so that each shall refer to some noun in the proper gender.

_____

_____

_____

2. Use the genitives *his, her, its* in the same way.

_____

_____

_____

3. Use *they* to refer to two masculine nouns

_____

   Use *they* to refer to two feminine nouns;

_____

   Use *they* to refer to two neuter nouns;

_____

   Use *they* to refer to two nouns of different gender.

_____

4. Use *I, my, thou, you* in sentences, and see if you can tell their gender.

_____

_____

_____

5. Use, in properly constructed sentences, *who, whose,* and *whom* to refer to persons;

_____

_____

   which to refer to animals;

_____

which to refer to things.

_____

Chapter 64: Plural of Nouns

Write in parallel columns the singular and the plural of:

a. Boy, girl, field, street, paper, book, pencil, brick, bell, door, hat, lesson, president, governor.

SINGULAR	PLURAL
boy	
girl	
field	
street	
paper	
book	
pencil	
brick	
bell	
door	
hat	
lesson	
president	
governor	

b. Fly, cry, reply, supply, ally, remedy, subsidy.

SINGULAR	PLURAL
fly	
cry	
reply	
supply	
ally	
remedy	
subsidy	

c. Toy, play, alley, donkey, ray, dray, survey, essay.

	SINGULAR	*PLURAL*
toy		
play		
alley		
donkey		
ray		
dray		
survey		

d. Calf, half, loaf, knife, wife, life.

	SINGULAR	*PLURAL*
calf		
half		
loaf		
knife		
wife		
life		

Compare your four lists, and see if you can frame a rule for the plural of:

(1) nouns that end in *-y* after a consonant,

_____

_____

_____

(2) nouns that end in *-y* after a vowel,

_____

_____

_____

(3) nouns like *calf* and *knife*.

_____

_____

_____

Chapter 65: Irregular Plurals, Part 1

There are no written exercises for this chapter.

Chapter 66: Irregular Plurals, Part 2

There are no written exercises for this chapter.

Chapter 67: Irregular Plurals, Part 3

I.

Use in sentences the **plurals** of these nouns:

1. man _____

2. fisherman_____

3. deer_____

4. sheep _____

5. child _____

6. ox _____

7. penny _____

8. Miss Clark _____

9. Mr. Ray_____

10. Mrs. Ray_____

11. cattle_____

12. horseman_____

13. tooth _____

14. German _____

15. mouse_____

16. foot _____

17. brother (*both plurals*)_____

_____

18. Master Wilson_____

19. Miss Atkins _____

20. handful_____

21. son-in-law _____

22. man-of-war _____

23. bluebird _____

24. handkerchief _____

Explain all the forms that you have used.

II.
Circle the plural nouns, and **write** the singular on the blank line.
Mention any peculiar plurals that you find.

1. Riches do many things. _____

2. Tears and lamentations were seen in almost every house. _____

    _____

3. The skipper boasted of his catch of fish. _____

4. With figs and plums and Persian dates they fed me. _____

5. The rest of my goods were returned me. _____

6. The sheep were browsing quietly on the low hills. _____

7. The Messrs. Bertram were very fine young men. _____

8. The admiration which the Misses Thomas felt for Mrs. Crawford was rapturous. _____

    _____

9. He drew out the nail with a pair of pincers. _____

10. His majesty marches northwards with a body of four thousand horse. _____

11. Flights of doves and lapwings were fluttering among the leaves. _____

12. Down fell the lady's thimble and scissors into the brook. _____

13. The Miss Blacks lived, according to the worldly phrase, out of the world. _____

    _____

14. The day after came the unfortunate news of the queen's death. _____

15. No person dined with the queen but the two princesses royal. _____

16. I cannot guess at the number of ships, but I think there must be several hundreds of sail. ___

    _____

17. The Miss Bertrams continued to exercise their memories. _____

18. Weavers, nailers, rope makers, artisans of every degree and calling, thronged forward to

    join the procession from every gloomy and narrow street. _____

    _____

19. Now all the youth of England are on fire. _____

20. Charles has some talent for writing verses. _____

Chapter 68: Personal Pronouns, Part 1

There are no written exercises for this chapter.

Chapter 69: Personal Pronouns, Part 2

I.

    (1) **Underline** the personal pronouns.

    (2) **Label** whether each is of the first **(1)**, the second **(2)**, or the third **(3)** person.

    (3) **Label** the gender **(M, F, N** or **M/F)** and number **(S, P)** of each.

1. He was my friend, faithful and just to me.

2. Mahomet accompanied his uncle on trading journeys.

3. Our Clifford was a happy youth.

4. And now, child, what art thou doing?

5. I think I can guess what you mean.

6. Then boast no more your mighty deeds!

7. Round him night resistless closes fast.

8. I was in the utmost astonishment, and roared so loud that they all ran back in fright.

9. She listens, but she cannot hear

    The foot of horse, the voice of man.

10. He hollowed a boat of the birchen bark,

    Which carried him off from shore.

11. At dead of night their sails were filled.

12. Men at some time are masters of their fates.

13. Here is a sick man that would speak with you.

14. Why should we yet our sail unfurl?

15. I once more thought of attempting to break my bonds.

16. Our fortune and fame had departed.

17. The Hawbucks came in their family coach, with the blood-red hand emblazoned all over it.

18. The spoken word cannot be recalled. It must go on its way for good or evil.

19. He saw the lake, and a meteor bright

    Quick over its surface played.

20. I have endeavored to solve this difficulty another way.

21. The military part of his life has furnished him with many adventures.

22. He ambled alongside the footpath on which they were walking, showing his discomfort by

    a twist of his neck every few seconds.

23. Our provisions held out well, our ship was stanch, and our crew all in good health; but we

    lay in the utmost distress for water.

24. Sweet day, so cool, so calm, so bright—

    The bridal of the earth and sky—

    The dew shall weep thy fall tonight,

    For thou must die.

25. Lend me thy cloak, Sir Thomas.

26. Captain Fluellen, you must come presently to the mines. The Duke of Gloucester would

    speak with you.

27. Madam, what should we do?

28. Worthy Macbeth, we stay upon your leisure.

29. Fair and noble hostess,

    We are your guest tonight.

II.
Identify the case of each personal pronoun in the sentences from Exercise I (reproduced below). **Label** nominative case with **N,** genitive case with **G,** and objective case with **O.**

1. He was my friend, faithful and just to me.

2. Mahomet accompanied his uncle on trading journeys.

3. Our Clifford was a happy youth.

4. And now, child, what art thou doing?

5. I think I can guess what you mean.

6. Then boast no more your mighty deeds!

7. Round him night resistless closes fast.

8. I was in the utmost astonishment, and roared so loud that they all ran back in fright.

9. She listens, but she cannot hear

   The foot of horse, the voice of man.

10. He hollowed a boat of the birchen bark,

    Which carried him off from shore.

11. At dead of night their sails were filled.

12. Men at some time are masters of their fates.

13. Here is a sick man that would speak with you.

14. Why should we yet our sail unfurl?

15. I once more thought of attempting to break my bonds.

16. Our fortune and fame had departed.

17. The Hawbucks came in their family coach, with the blood-red hand emblazoned all over it.

18. The spoken word cannot be recalled. It must go on its way for good or evil.

19. He saw the lake, and a meteor bright

    Quick over its surface played.

20. I have endeavored to solve this difficulty another way.

21. The military part of his life has furnished him with many adventures.

22. He ambled alongside the footpath on which they were walking, showing his discomfort by

    a twist of his neck every few seconds.

23. Our provisions held out well, our ship was stanch, and our crew all in good health; but we lay in the utmost distress for water.

24. Sweet day, so cool, so calm, so bright—

   The bridal of the earth and sky—

   The dew shall weep thy fall tonight,

   For thou must die.

25. Lend me thy cloak, Sir Thomas.

26. Captain Fluellen, you must come presently to the mines. The Duke of Gloucester would speak with you.

27. Madam, what should we do?

28. Worthy Macbeth, we stay upon your leisure.

29. Fair and noble hostess,

   We are your guest tonight.

III.
In these sentences from chapter 4, Exercise I, **underline** each pronoun and:
   (1) **Label** the person **(1, 2,** or **3)**,
   (2) **Label** the number **(S** or **P)**,
   (3) **Label** gender **(M, F, N,** or **M/F)**
   (4) **Label** the case **(N, G, O)**

This exercise is called "parsing" words.

1. A number of young people were assembled in the music room.

2. He leads towards Rome a band of warlike Goths.

3. By ten o'clock the whole party were assembled at the Park.

4. Have I not reason to look pale and dead?

5. People were terrified by the force of their own imagination.

6. The Senate has letters from the general.

7. You misuse the reverence of your place.

8. There is hardly any place, or any company, where you may not gain knowledge if you please.

9. Here comes another troop to seek for you.

10. Their mastiffs are of unmatchable courage.

11. Our family dined in the field, and we sat, or rather reclined, round a temperate repast.

12. Our society will not break up, but we shall settle in some other place.

13. Let nobody blame him; his scorn I approve.

14. The Senate have concluded

    To give this day a crown to mighty Caesar.

15. He is banished, as enemy to the people and his country.

16. Society has been called the happiness of life.

17. His army is a ragged multitude

    Of hinds and peasants, rude and merciless.

18. There is a great difference between knowledge and wisdom.

19. All the country in a general voice cried hate upon him.

20. The king hath called his Parliament.

21. Let all the number of the stars give light to thy fair way!

IV.

Use these personal pronouns in sentences of your own:

me _____

he _____

you (objective)_____

him _____

she_____

us_____

ye _____

thou_____

my_____

mine _____

thee_____

its_____

yours_____

our _____

I _____

ours_____

their _____

it (nominative) _____

thine _____

his _____

her (objective) _____

it (objective)_____

theirs_____

her (genitive)_____

we _____

thy_____

your _____

you (nominative)_____

hers_____

they_____

them _____

Chapter 70: Nominative and Objective Case

Underline the substantives that are subjects and **label** them **N** for nominative case.
Circle the substantives that are objects and **label** them **O** for objective case.

1. Forth on his fiery steed betimes he rode.

2. A thick forest lay near the city.

3. When they met, they made a surly stand.

4. It is true, hundreds, yea thousands of families fled away at this last plague.

5. Some of these rambles led me to great distances.

6. When the moonlight nights returned, we used to venture into the desert.

7. He loaded a great wagon with hay.

8. With her two brothers this fair lady dwelt.

9. The lord of the castle in wrath arose.

10. The fair breeze blew, the white foam flew,

    The furrow followed free;

    We were the first that ever burst

    Into that silent sea.

11. A dense fog shrouded the landscape.

12. How he blessed this little Polish lady!

Chapter 71: Predicate Nominative

Review the exercises from chapters 43-46. Be sure that you recognize the difference between predicate nominatives, predicate adjectives, and direct objects.

Chapter 72: Nominative in Exclamations

I.

Review vocatives and chapter 15, Exercise II, which is reproduced below.
In each of the following sentences **underline** the subject **once** and the predicate **twice**.
Label also any vocative nouns which the sentences contain with a **V**.

1. O learned sir,
   You and your learning I revere.

2. The good old man
   Means no offense, sweet lady!

3. Goodbye! Drive on, coachman.

4. Why, Sir John, my face does you no harm.

5. Good cousin, give me audience for a while.

6. Yours is the prize, victorious prince.

7. "Wake, Allan-bane," aloud she cried
   To the old minstrel by her side.

8. Bid adieu, my sad heart, bid adieu to thy peace.

9. My dear little cousin, what can be the matter?

10. Come, Evening, once again, season of peace!

11. Plain truth, dear Murray, needs no flowers of speech.

12. Permit me now, Sir William, to address myself personally to you.

13. Go, my dread lord, to your great-grandsire's tomb.

14. Why do you stay so long, my lords of France?

15. My pretty cousins, you mistake me much.

16. Come on, Lord Hastings. Will you go with me?

17. O Romeo, Romeo, brave Mercutio's dead.

18. I will avenge this insult, noble queen.

19. O friend, I seek a harborage for the night.

20. My lord, I saw three bandits by the rock.

21. Father! thy days have passed in peace.

II.

Underline all the **vocatives** and **circle** all the **exclamatory nominatives**.

1. Roll on, thou deep and dark-blue ocean, roll!

2. Weapons! Arms! What's the matter here?

3. Tartar, and Saphi, and Turcoman,

    Strike your tents and throng to the van.

4. Awake! what ho, Brabantio! thieves! thieves! thieves!

5. She, poor wretch! for grief can speak no more.

6. Fair daffodils, we weep to see

    You haste away so soon.

7. Weep no more, woeful shepherds, weep no more.

8. O father! I am young and very happy.

9. O wonder! how many goodly creatures are there here!

10. Milton! thou should'st be living at this hour.

11. Liberty! freedom! Tyranny is dead!

12. Farewell, ye dungeons dark and strong.

III.

Write sentences containing the following nouns:

      (1) as vocatives,

      (2) as exclamatory nominatives.

Use an adjective with each noun.

Mary _____

_____

boy _____

_____

hunter_____

_____

Rover _____

_____

Scott _____

_____

woman _____

_____

friend _____

_____

comrades _____

_____

king _____

_____

sailor _____

_____

Harry _____

_____

winter _____

_____

rain _____

_____

father _____

_____

brother _____

_____

IV.

Analyze the sentences in II.

    (1) **Underline** the complete subject **once** and complete predicate **twice**. (Remember that vocatives and exclamatory nominatives should not be included in the complete subject or predicate; they stand alone.)

    (2) **Label** simple subject with **S** and simple predicate with **Pred.**

    (3) **Place** parentheses around phrases and brackets around clauses.

    (4) **Label** vocatives with **V** and exclamatory nominatives with **E.**

    (5) **Label** modifiers (adverbs **Adv**, adjectives **Adj**, adverb clauses **Adv**, adjective clauses **Adj**).

1. Roll on, thou deep and dark-blue ocean, roll!

2. Weapons! Arms! What's the matter here?

3. Tartar, and Saphi, and Turcoman, strike your tents and throng to the van.

4. Awake! what ho, Brabantio! thieves! thieves! thieves!

5. She, poor wretch! for grief can speak no more.

6. Fair daffodils, we weep to see

    You haste away so soon.

7. Weep no more, woeful shepherds, weep no more.

8. O father! I am young and very happy.

9. O wonder! how many goodly creatures are there here!

10. Milton! thou should'st be living at this hour.

11. Liberty! freedom! Tyranny is dead!

12. Farewell, ye dungeons dark and strong.

Chapter 72: Additional Review Exercises

Underline the nominatives (all nouns or pronouns in nominative case) in the following sentences.

Parse them with the following steps:

(1) **Write** nominative *class* to which it belongs (subject with **Sub**, predicate nominative with **PN**, vocative with **V**, exclamatory with **E**, appositive with **A**),

(2) **Write** the gender (**M, F, N,** or **M/F**), and

(3) **Write** the number (**S** or **P**).

The first one is done for you.

1. The <u>moonbeams</u> streamed on the tall tower of St. Mark.

moonbeams: Sub, N, P

2. Their parents were respectable farmers.

3. A cold chill ran through Sam's veins.

4. The crowd was dispersed, and several of the rioters were slain.

5. Howling Winter fled afar.

6. Poor Cinderella! Her life was very hard.

7. Captain Brown and his two daughters lived in a small house on the outskirts of the village.

8. O ye wild groves, O, where is now your bloom?

9. Auspicious Hope, in thy sweet garden grow

_____

   Wreaths for each toil, a charm for every woe.

_____

10. The haymakers were at work in the fields, and the perfume of the new-mown hay brought

    with it the recollection of my home.

_____

11. My uncle listened with inward impatience while the little marquis descanted, with his

    usual fire and vivacity, on the achievements of his ancestors, whose portraits hung along

    the wall.

_____

_____

12. Every visitor who arrived after nightfall was challenged from a loophole or from a

    barricaded window.

_____

13. The Romans were, in their origin, banditti.

_____

14. Her father dwelt where yonder castle shines

_____

   O'er clust'ring trees and terrace-mantling vines.

_____

15. Delay not, Caesar. Read it instantly.

_____

Chapter 73: Genitive or Possessive Case

I.

Attach a noun to the genitive of each of these names.

Thus,

        Smith   Smith's stable

Jones _____

Thomas_____

Gibbs _____

Cyrus _____

Charles_____

Caesar_____

Julius_____

Mr. Converse_____

Mr. Conners_____

Mrs. Ross _____

Charles Foss _____

Antonius _____

Brutus_____

Cassius_____

Mr. Anthony Brooks_____

J. T. Fields_____

Romulus_____

Remus _____

Mr. Strangways_____

Mrs. Smithers _____

Matthew_____

John Matthews _____

Dr. Morris _____

Maurice _____

Lord Douglas _____

Dr. Ellis_____

James _____

Francis _____

Frances_____

Eunice_____

Felix _____

Rose _____

II.

Use in sentences the phrases that you have made in Exercise I.

1. _____

2. _____

3. _____

4. _____

5. _____

6. _____

7. _____

8. _____

9. _____

10. _____

11. _____

12. _____

13. _____

14. _____

15. _____

16. _____

17. _____

18. _____

19. _____

20. _____

21. _____

22. _____

23. _____

24. _____

25. _____

26. _____

27. _____

28. _____

29. _____

30. _____

31. _____

32. _____

33. _____

III.

Review chapter 35, Exercise II.

IV.

Attach a noun to the genitive, singular **and** plural, of each of these words (as in I, above). The first one is done for you.

horse ___*horse's bridle*___ ___*horses' bridle*___ _____

man_____

woman_____

child_____

fish_____

gentleman_____

deer_____

sheep_____

bird_____

wolf_____

calf_____

tiger_____

snake_____

badger_____

fly_____

spy_____

turkey_____

donkey_____

ally_____

V.

In the sentences from chapter 33, Exercises I and IV, reproduced below, **underline** all the genitives and all the *of*-phrases and **draw an arrow** to what noun or pronoun each belongs.

<u>Chapter 33, I</u>

1. The emperor's palace is in the center of the city, where the two great streets meet.

2. Oliver's education began when he was about three years old.

3. Caesar scorns the poet's lays.

4. The silver light, with quivering glance,

   Played on the water's still expanse.

5. Here on this beach a hundred years ago,

   Three children of three houses, Annie Lee,

   The prettiest little damsel in the port,

   And Philip Ray, the miller's only son,

   And Enoch Arden, a rough sailor's lad,

   Made orphan by a winter shipwreck, played

   Among the waste and lumber of the shore.

6. It is not the greatness of a man's means that makes him independent, so much as the smallness of his wants.

7. In faith and hope the world will disagree,

   But all mankind's concern is charity.

8. The jester's speech made the duke laugh.

9. A man's nature runs either to herbs or weeds.

<u>Chapter 33, IV</u>

1. The monarch's wrath began to rise.

2. They err who imagine that this man's courage was ferocity.

3. Two years' travel in distant and barbarous countries has accustomed me to bear privations.

4. Hark! hark! the lark at heaven's gate sings.

5. Portia dressed herself and her maid in men's apparel.

6. He waved his huntsman's cap on high.

7. The Porters' visit was all but over.

8. The ladies' colds kept them at home all the evening.

9. The crags repeat the ravens' croak.

10. Farmer Grove's house is on fire!

11. The Major paced the terrace in front of the house for his two hours' constitutional walk.

VI.

In each sentence in Exercise V substitute, orally, an *of*-phrase for a genitive or a genitive for an *of*-phrase, as the case may be, and tell whether the sentence as thus changed is good or bad English.

Chapter 74: Case of Appositives

I.

Review the exercises from chapter 37, reproduced below. Remember that appositives take the same case as the substantive which they define.

Underline the appositives. **Label** the case of each appositive, **N** for nominative case, **O** for objective case.

Chapter 37, I

1. Mr. Jones, the _____, is building a house for me.

2. Have you seen Rover, my _____, anywhere?

3. We saw animals of all kinds in the menagerie, _____, _____,

   and _____.

4. Chapman, the _____ of the team, broke his collar bone.

5. My new kite, _____ from my uncle, is caught in the tree.

6. Washington, the _____ of the United States, is on the Potomac.

7. Who has met my young friend _____ today?

8. Charles I, _____ of England, was beheaded in 1649.

9. Washington, the _____ of his country, was born in 1732.

10. The sultan was fond of tiger-hunting, a dangerous _____.

Chapter 37, II

1. An Englishwoman, the wife of one of the officers, was sitting on the battlements with her

   child in her arms.

2. I went to visit Mr. Hobbes, the famous philosopher.

3. We were hopeful boys, all three of us.

4. Spring, the sweet Spring, is the year's pleasant king.

5. Then forth they all out of their baskets drew

Great store of flowers, the honor of the field.

6. He was speedily summoned to the apartment of his captain, the Lord Crawford.

7. No rude sound shall reach thine ear,

   Armor's clang and war-steed champing.

8. And thus spake on that ancient man,

   The bright-eyed mariner.

9. There lived at no great distance from this stronghold a farmer, a bold and stout man, whose name was Binnock.

II.
Underline the appositives.
Label the case of each (nominative with **N**, objective with **O**)

1. I visited my old friend and fellow-traveler, Mr. Henshaw.

2. At length the day dawned, — that dreadful day.

3. 'Twas where the madcap duke his uncle kept.

4. So off they scampered, man and horse.

5. The north wind, that welcome visitor, freshened the air.

6. I see him yet, the princely boy!

7. His prayer he saith, this patient, holy man.

8. The vices of authority are chiefly four: delays, corruption, roughness, and facility.

9. 'T is past, that melancholy dream!

10. Campley, a friend of mine, came by.

11. The mayor, an aged man, made an address.

12. He lent me his only weapon, a sword.

13. Captain William Robinson, a Cornishman, commander of the "Hopewell," a stout ship of three hundred tons, came to my house.

III.

Analyze each of the sentences from Exercise II, which are reproduced below.

(1) **Underline** complete subject **once** and complete predicate **twice**.

(2) **Label** simple subject with **S** and simple predicate with **Pred.**

(3) **Place** parentheses around phrases and appositives, brackets around clauses.

(4) **Label** vocatives with **V** and exclamatory nominatives with **E.**

(5) **Label** modifiers (adverbs with **Adv**, adjectives with **Adj**, adverb clauses with **Adv**, adjective clauses with **Adj**). Remember that appositives are identified as adjective phrases.

1. I visited my old friend and fellow-traveler, Mr. Henshaw.

2. At length the day dawned, — that dreadful day.

3. 'Twas where the madcap duke his uncle kept.

4. So off they scampered, man and horse.

5. The north wind, that welcome visitor, freshened the air.

6. I see him yet, the princely boy!

7. His prayer he saith, this patient, holy man.

8. The vices of authority are chiefly four: delays, corruption, roughness, and facility.

9. 'T is past, that melancholy dream!

10. Campley, a friend of mine, came by.

11. The mayor, an aged man, made an address.

12. He lent me his only weapon, a sword.

13. Captain William Robinson, a Cornishman, commander of the "Hopewell," a stout ship of three hundred tons, came to my house.

Chapter 75: Indirect Object

I.

Fill in each blank with an indirect object (noun or pronoun).

1. My sister gave _____ a book.

2. A deserter brought _____ news of the battle.

3. The king granted _____ a pension of a hundred pounds.

4. Alfred will show _____ his collection of postage stamps.

5. The governor paid _____ the reward.

6. The prisoner told _____ the whole story.

7. De Quincey's father left _____ a large sum of money.

8. Our teacher granted _____ our request.

9. Can such conduct give _____ any satisfaction?

10. His indulgent father forgave _____ his many faults.

11. The grocer refused _____ credit.

12. The surly porter refused _____ permission to enter the building.

II.

Circle all the direct objects that you find, and **underline** the phrases in which the idea of the indirect object is expressed by means of *to*. **Draw an arrow** from the direct object to the indirect object.

1. He by will bequeathed his lands to me.

2. To Mortimer will I declare these tidings.

3. He has told all his troubles to you.

4. Entrust your message to her.

5. Do you give attention to my words?

6. The judges awarded the prize to Oliver.

7. Do you ascribe this drama to Shakespeare?

8. Show the drawing to your teacher.

9. The scout made his report to the officer.

III.

Make ten sentences containing the following verbs, with both a direct **and** an indirect object:

1. sold _____

2. told _____

3. pays _____

4. sends_____

5. will bring _____

6. have brought_____

7. had shown_____

8. fetches _____

9. denied_____

10. lent _____

IV.

In the following sentences:

      (1) **underline** the subject **once** and the predicate **twice**,

      (2) **circle** the direct objects,

      (3) **draw an arrow** from the direct object to the indirect objects.

1. I shall assign you the post of danger and of renown.

2. The king ordered him a small present and dismissed him.

3. The thoughts of the day gave my mind employment for the whole night.

4. Miss Pratt gave Uncle Adam a jog on the elbow.

5. The king made me a present.

6. I will bring you certain news from Shrewsbury.

7. I will deny thee nothing.

8. Fetch me the hat and rapier in my cell.

9. Forgive us our sins!

10. My father gave him welcome.

11. I will not lend thee a penny.

12. The mayor in courtesy showed me the castle.

13. I shall tell you a pretty tale.

14. Vouchsafe me one fair look.

15. The reading of those volumes afforded me much amusement.

16. I have occasioned her some confusion, and, for the moment, a little resentment.

17. He'll make her two or three fine speeches, and then she'll be perfectly contented.

18. Voltaire, who was then in England, sent him a letter of consolation.

19. The evening had afforded Edmund little pleasure.

20. Mrs. St. Clair here wished the happy pair good morning.

A. Punctuation Practice Exercises

Copy the following sentences and make all capitalization and punctuation corrections.

1. it will be midnight said the coachman before we arrive at our inn

_____

_____

2. we give thee heart and hand

_____

    our glorious native land

_____

3. yet though destruction sweep those lovely plains

_____

_____

    rise fellow-men our country yet remains

_____

4. after a dreadful night of anxiety perplexity and peril the darkness slowly disappeared

_____

_____

5. as he that lives longest lives but a little while every man may be certain that he has no time

    to waste

_____

_____

6. at its western side is a deep ravine or valley through which a small stream rushes

_____

_____

B. Punctuation Practice Exercises

Copy the following sentences and make all capitalization and punctuation corrections.

1. the vision of sir launfal was written by james russell lowell

2. will not your trip to bath afford you an opportunity to visit us at weston

3. that is my brother said jack

4. dr adams the eminent surgeon took charge of the case

5. we ran on the dogs pursuing us until we reached the bridge

6. a quotation especially if it is a long quotation should always be to the point

7. she hastened downstairs ordered the servants to arm themselves with the weapons first at hand placed herself at their head,and returned immediately

C. Punctuation Practice Exercises

Copy the following sentences and make all capitalization and punctuation corrections. The selected sentences have missing capitals and punctuation. *Hint:* There are five sentences in the selection.

the boys were glad to find a blazing fire awaiting them upon their return to the red lion carl and his party were there first soon afterward peter and jacob came in they had inquired in vain concerning dr boekman all they could ascertain was that he had been seen in haarlem that morning --MARY MAPES, HANS BRINKER OR THE SILVER SKATES

_____

_____

_____

_____

_____

_____

_____

_____

_____

_____

_____

_____

_____

_____

_____

D. Punctuation Practice Exercises

Copy the following selection and supply the proper capitals and punctuation marks. *Hint:* There are four sentences in the paragraph. Be sure to punctuate dates and numerals properly.

on january 2 we had made 11340 miles or 5250 french leagues since our starting-point in the japan seas before the ships head stretched the dangerous shores of the coral sea on the northeast coast of australia our boat lay along some miles from the redoubtable bank on which cooks vessel was lost june 10 1770 the boat in which cook was struck on a rock and if it did not sink it was owing to a piece of the coral that was broken by the shock and fixed itself in the broken keel -JULES VERNE, TWENTY THOUSAND LEAGUES UNDER THE SEA

Made in the USA
Coppell, TX
24 June 2023

18447727R00103